1

Trump

The Biography

Trump

The Biography

From Businessman to 45th President of
the United States

Insight and Analysis into the Life of
Donald J. Trump

J.R. MacGregor

Trump – The Biography

Published by CAC Publishing LLC

ISBN 978-1-950010-39-4 paperback

ISBN 978-1-950010-38-7 eBook

Table of Contents

Introduction

However we relate to a person, however great we think they are, or, consequently, how horrible, that person is just the manifestation of the sum of their past and the influences of their current environment. The accounting of those manifestations and the audit of those influences taken through the eyes of one's own experiences gives us an understanding and opinion of that person.

The more their words and actions affect us adversely in reality or in thought, the easier it becomes to place a distance between ourselves and that person. The more their actions or our impressions of those actions sits well within our psyche, the deeper we want to be entrenched in that person's orbit.

Politicians are an interesting group of people, but they are just people not too different from everyone else you see around you. The only difference is that they know how to manage your perception of them. The problem with managing perceptions is that the person in question ends up appealing only to a crowd that is susceptible to that management or the crowd that likes the persona and position that the person adopts.

It's not that complicated. If you want the vote of someone who appreciates the color blue and is put at ease by it, then you are going to always be wearing blue. If you want to be voted for by someone, or a large group of people, who strongly believe that the dilution of American liberties, security, and prosperity is caused by immigrants, legal or otherwise, then you make that your cause and speak loudly until all of them hear you clearly. That is just common sense. You become what your voter, your base wants and likes even when that is not really you.

It becomes even simpler if you follow this argument down through its logical development. Politicians are not the same as statesmen. American politics has not seen a statesman since the Reagan era. What we have seen since the '90s are politicians saying exactly what the people want to hear. The widespread response to that has been one of distrust. When Donald Trump came on the scene, he had altered the expectations that people applied to him. He had already spent the last three decades building a reputation as a billionaire playboy philanthropist—the Tony Stark of this reality and our generation.

Is that so bad? Well, not really. The American system of democracy deserves a little background to understand the state of politics in today's world. It was clearly articulated in Thomas Paine's *Common Sense*.

In that booklet, Paine laid out what it means to

have an elected government. To paraphrase his analogy, he talks about representative government as a way for people to choose elected officials to represent them at various levels of government. It is not a popularity contest.

He starts off by painting a picture where there are just a few people in a new country. They have shared responsibilities, and they all come together to look after that shared responsibility. If they need to build roads, they come together to build the roads. If they have to pay for new services, they all chip in and pay for them.

It's all easy to do when only a few people are in this imaginary new country. As the number of people in that new country grows, these meetings where they come together start to get unruly. As time goes by and the island of ten becomes an island of a million, it makes no sense that the one million inhabitants come together to meet; in fact, it would be impossible. So they decide to manage common issues by representation. They decide to divide the population by location and elect one person to represent the population in that location. So now they have one person to represent perhaps a hundred thousand people in specific parts of the new country.

This person is a professional representative. He is there to make the voice of the population in his constituency heard. The people of that district or constituency come together and decide who will represent them. Just like a sports agent who represents an athlete in negotiating his terms, the representative is there to do what is in the best interest of the people he represents.

To make the point a little clearer and more relevant to the subject of this book, we must ask ourselves the following question. Does it matter that our psychiatrist battles the same psychological issue that we may face? To put it bluntly, does our lawyer need to be insane to plead insanity on our behalf? Does it matter that our dentist suffers the same orthodontic problems that we do? Does our priest need to be married to be able to dole out marital advice? The answer is no. It is not practical for a professional we engage to have the same problems that we do. Only simple minds may think so.

To take that one step further, we ask ourselves what happens if my representative is exactly like me and has the same amount of land and cattle that I do. Does that now make him my perfect representative? If so, does that now not make him the wrong representative for someone else in our constituency?

The point is that the representative Thomas Paine described in his analogy does not need to resemble the members of his constituency; rather, that person only needs to understand their aggregate needs.

The representative is allowed to alter his point of view on topics. He may personally dislike Policy X but is welcome to support it when he finds that the majority of his constituency want it or will benefit by it. He is not being duplicitous. He is being professional. It takes a higher mind to be able to put aside his own beliefs and fight for the beliefs of others.

Donald Trump is a transactional person. He does things based on transactions, and he follows through on them. Because of this he is also someone who relies on contracts. These and the contractual obligations that arise from them are transactional by nature. Trump's election was a contract—a valid one. He agreed to fight for the policies dear to those who supported him, and they elected him.

Just because Trump didn't in the past share the same beliefs as his voters in the present does not mean he can't fight for them now. His past support, or lack of it, does not disqualify him from representing the people who do as long as he fights for what they want him to fight for. If, on the other hand, he promised them something they wanted and they voted for him because of that but he went back to championing his own beliefs, then that would be breaking the contract that exists between them. He won't do that.

Whether or not he believes in the same values as the evangelical constituency he represents is wholly unimportant. What matters is that he represent the values of those who voted for him—his base.

Some will make lots of noise about the morals and behavior of a president, but this logic is faulty. As the Trump base has rightly proven, the representative of the people does not have to be someone of impeccable moral standing. That person just needs to be someone who fights for the will of the people they represent.

Who his paramour of the day is, what he grabs, or how many wives he has is really not anyone's business as long as he gets the job done. Do you question your pilot's habits or his proclivities? Would you deplane if you found out he was on his third marriage and had a girlfriend while his third wife was busy with their newborn baby? No. You would still take the flight and go about your business

The same is true here.

What is lost in today's conversation is that people go to the polls to elect a representative who will do their job of representation. They are not electing a statesman. Statesmen are made, not elected.

With that being said, it is incumbent upon us to remember that it is not the job of the person who is elected to office to be the role model for the youth of the day. In fact, a politician should never be a person's role model. If that person rises to the level of being statesmen because by virtue of his individuality or the unique contribution he advances the constituency he is elected in to rise so high that it deserves accolades, then so be it. Just know that many people who are not elected go on to become statesmen.

The only metric that a person should be elected on is whether or not he or she will represent your interests. Once their term is over, you have only one question: Did he or she do the job you sent them there to do? In Trump's case, the answer would be in the affirmative.

It is as simple as that. What their grades were, how they made their money, how many affairs they had do not matter. To make it so, whether it was Kennedy and his mistress, Clinton and his affairs, or any other White House occupant who extended their activities beyond the confines of their marital confines has no bearing on their ability to do for us what we elected them to do. No one should treat the president as a role model for themselves or their children.

Having said that, the biography that takes shape under the cover of this Introduction will be one that lays out the information regarding the subject within the appropriate context. The American president is, after all, a politician, and the role of a politician is to do what his constituents want. At this stage of the American journey, a significant number of people want certain things, and President Trump has stepped in to provide it for them. That is how democracy works.

Some aspects of his life may come across as salacious, but it is not intended to be, and some may come across as arrogant and brutish, but that is not intended either. The point is to give a clear revelation of the events in his life that have made him the perfect person to fill the role as POTUS.

We will look at three stages of this man's life: his ancestry, his life before the campaign for the presidency, and his recent life. If one looks closely, it becomes apparent that he has two sides. One is the real Donald Trump that is kept away from the rest of the world, and the other is the veneer that he wears to face the world.

Chapter 1 The Crossing

The 1800s was the first full century of the American nation. Having just gained its independence in 1776, the different states were still in the process of coming together under one federal government.

Until the first presidential election in 1789, there was no constitution, no elected officials, and the states were only united in name. It was only after the first presidential election and the first congressional elections that the Senate was established—selected by each state's assemblies.

With the lack of a government between 1776 and 1789 and a few years thereafter, there was nothing to regulate actions and conflicts within the states. A person committing a crime in one state could easily cross the border and be outside the jurisdiction of consequence for his actions. It was truly a "cowboy-esque" state of affairs.

It was easy to start fresh in this new land. Whether it was the pious man in search of freedom to practice his beliefs or the sinner looking for reprieve, the new America was the shining beacon of hope, which blanketed the world with its invitation, and many took heed.

By the time the 1800s came around, America

was just starting to get under way. Washington, his cabinet, and Congress were busy laying out the framework of government and how the country would organize itself. It was a busy period, and everyone was making it up as they went along. They didn't know what they wanted as much as they knew what they didn't want.

One reason why President Washington remains such an iconic figure is not because he holds the historical place of being the first president, but because he molded the presidency and by extension, the country, to his values and ideals. The American presidency was shaped by him and reflected his spirit. Much of how any individual discharges the duties of his office is not codified in law but forged in practice and convention.

While the machinery of politics kept grinding, the country was not as economically stable as it could have been with more people and was more diverse. There weren't enough people in the country to mine, farm, and build. Industries could not grow, farms could not expand, and lands could not be opened up. Many resources were available in the West, but there was no one to bring life to it.

Thus, the country turned to immigration. It was opened to people all around the world. America was open for business. A pipeline of diaspora followed that reached all corners of the world. People came from Ireland, Scotland, Germany, and everywhere else imaginable. The world heeded that call so eloquently expressed by Emma Lazarus,

"Not like the brazen giant of Greek fame,

With conquering limbs astride from land to land;

Here at our sea-washed, sunset gates shall stand

A mighty woman with a torch, whose flame

Is the imprisoned lightning, and her name

Mother of Exiles. From her beacon-hand

Glows world-wide welcome; her mild eyes command

The air-bridged harbor that twin cities frame.

"Keep, ancient lands, your storied pomp!" cries she

With silent lips. "Give me your tired, your poor,

Your huddled masses yearning to breathe free,

The wretched refuse of your teeming shore.

Send these, the homeless, tempest-tossed to me,

I lift my lamp beside the golden door!"

Lazarus had written that sonnet as part of the

movement to raise funds for the Statue of Liberty. It was by no means an invitation, but it is reminiscent of the mind-set that was pervasive in a country that was so far ahead of its time in terms of its founding principles.

The plaque was installed at the base of the Statue of Liberty in 1903. The statue itself was built in 1885 as a gift from France and shipped to the U.S. It was erected on Liberty Island (then known as Bedloe's Island) the following year in time for the centenary celebrations. It was dedicated in October 1886 by President Grover Cleveland.

When Friedrich Trumpf arrived in New York the previous month, he became one of the first immigrants to be welcomed by the statue that symbolized liberty, standing more than three hundred feet high in the otherwise flat terrain of New York harbor. The statue was a comforting sight for all those who had set on that long journey across the North Atlantic. When he left Bremen and sailed along the Weser before reaching the North Sea, one of the last things he would have seen was the Bremen Statue, a fifteenth-century soldier of Charlemagne—a symbol of freedom and liberty.

The key to his departure was a function of two factors—much the same as it was for almost everyone else. The first was the invitation that was broadcast to the Old World with the enticement of opportunities. New frontiers were opened up by offering land in return for emigrating to the New World. That was the pull.

The second was the push from the Old World. There was widespread poverty, from famines and displacement of revolutions, and there was also religious and cultural persecution. The push-pull effect ramped up the rates of immigration for people with dreams as diverse as their cultures, getting on steamships and deathships just to make it to this new land. From such families as the Vanderbilts to the Carnegies and the Fords, hundreds of thousands of immigrants descended on America.

Europe was a major source of the population for young America. Germany had a large share of the waves of immigration that reached American shores. Most set sail from Bremen or Bremerhaven. Bremen was located deep inland and served the landlocked area of inner Bavaria, moving goods and people in and out by way of the Weser River that emptied into the North Sea.

The port city of Bremen is about 350 miles from Trumpf's village of birth and where he lived. There were two ports in Bavaria around the time of his departure—Bremen and Bremerhaven. Bremen was the original port, and Bremerhaven was built to replace it. If you were an immigrant who left Germany in the early 1800s or earlier, you would have left from Bremen, but then the Weser River that leads from Bremen out to the ocean started to accumulate silt, preventing ships from reaching the inland port. This prompted the mayor of the city to commission the construction of a new port at the mouth of the river at Bremerhaven. For a period of time, Bremerhaven became the point of departure for most North Europeans.

Because the port of Bremen was still highly functional except for the silt, effort was made to dredge the riverbed, clean up the silt, and deepen the river. Once that was done, Bremen was revitalized and put back into use. Until that happened, passengers could travel by carriage to Bremerhaven or board a barge from Bremen to Bremerhaven and set sail from there.

For many soon-to-be German-Americans, the day they left Bremen/Bremerhaven would be the last time they would ever see Bavaria or even Europe for that matter. Most immigrants had only enough money to pay for passage, and they would spend the rest of their lives working to survive and raise their family in America. Only a few returned to their hometowns decades later carrying a new passport but speaking the old tongue.

Many churches and hotels are found in the city today, just as there were almost one hundred and fifty years ago. Many of the Bavarians who trickled into the city would spend their time at the churches—a place to steal their hearts and warm their families. It was a chance to say good-bye to a land they and their ancestors had known all their lives. They were leaving all that was familiar at home and going to a life that had nothing in common with what they knew. From the food they ate to the air they breathed and the words they heard, it was all going to be completely different.

For young Trumpf, it was a little different. He had arrived in Bremen a few days before he set sail without the permission or knowledge of his mother. She woke up one morning to a letter on the kitchen table informing her that he had left for Bremen.

It was a 350-mile journey from Kallstadt to Bremen. That was the first leg of his trip. Evidence suggests that Trumpf was about fifteen or sixteen when he left home and his mother. He found his way to Bremen through a myriad of transportation modes, including carriage and train, but he didn't have enough money to make it by train for the entire distance, so it took him about two weeks to get there.

The age he left home is not entirely certain. Much of his personal information was gleaned from his passport application and entries made during his immigration stop in New York, but there are discrepancies between these and the logs of the shipping company that operated the vessel he listed.

Records indicate that he boarded the *SS Eider*. It was the summer of 1886. This ship was full to capacity, and the journey wasn't pleasant, especially down in steerage where Trumpf spent his days. The trip took anywhere from four to six weeks to arrive in New York, and the only sunlight and sea breeze he would get was when he went up on deck on preallocated dates and times. Other than that he was in the berths down below under the watermark.

He indicates in his passport application a few years after becoming a U.S. citizen that he arrived in 1885. If we look at his arrival records at the port of entry, it lists Freid and that he was sixteen years of age when he arrived. That's how we date his date of birth back to 1869, but that same passport application lists the *SS Eider* as the ship he arrived on, but the *SS Eider* didn't travel to America in 1885 according to emigrant ship records.

Assuming that it is just an error, what we do know is that he was between fifteen and sixteen years of age when he landed, and it was either 1885 or 1886. What we do know for certain, however, is that he came from a family of winegrowers. It was not a rich existence and is not to be misunderstood that vineyards and wineries were lucrative businesses they are today, but back then it was just about a stable living. Trumpf had a number of siblings, older and younger than he was, but he was the weakest of the lot. What he lacked in physical strength and academic intelligence, however, he made up for in wit and charm. He could sweet-talk anyone into anything.

Just after he was born, his father, Johannes Trumpf, the proprietor of the winery, became ill. He contracted emphysema and other complications arising from his work. He was bedridden for a decade during which time the rest of his family worked the fields and lived on what they could, spending most of their income trying to cure Johannes. Once they were all out of money, they borrowed more in pursuit of a cure, but he eventually died and left the family in dire straits. Of all the children in the family, Frederich was the only one who didn't work because of his own poor health.

Instead of having to pay his way like his siblings, Trumpf's mother sent him to trade school located in an adjacent neighborhood in Kallstadt so that he could make his way as he got older. This move by his mother turned out to be wise, as his skills as a barber helped him make his way when he landed in New York.

Kallstadt is a town located southeast of Cologne and northwest of Stuttgart in today's Germany. Back then it was part of the Kingdom of Bavaria. Even today, this simple town has a small population of just over a thousand people, with a population density similar to that of a rural town in Kansas.

Everyone knew everyone else. As small as this town was, it had a great share of notable names on the world stage in the years to come. The first was Heinz, and the second was Drumpf. Both would go on in the next century to become towering names in American industry and imagination.

Friedrich Drumpf was born March 14, 1869, according to his U.S. passport application form. He was born in the outskirts of Kallstadt village in the Rhineland-Palatinate to Johannes Drumpf. The spelling of the family name should not be distracting, however, because spellings change over time, and most names were Americanized as immigrants were processed through immigration points during arrival.

At the time he left Bavaria, Friedrich's last name was pronounced "Droomp" by the locals. When he arrived in Castle Garden, New York, the ledger for arrivals has him listed as Fried Trumpf. It isn't clear why there was a mild change, but it may have been in misunderstanding pronunciation; nonetheless, Drumpf had become Trumpf.

Castle Garden was the original port of entry before Congress constructed Ellis Island in 1892. It was common at the time for immigrants to alter how their names were pronounced, or the immigration officers would do it for them. Names were truncated, altered for easier pronunciation, or just completely changed, facilitating the start of a new life.

The Drumpf family had set their sights on America for some time. Friedrich's older sister had married Friedrich, a shoemaker in Kallstadt, and emigrated to America as soon as they could save enough for passage from Bremen. They had left a few years earlier. Once they arrived, they settled in New York and sent word back to

Germany that life was good. This, along with other stories young Friedrich had heard up to that point, enticed his interest in this new country.

Another pressing matter also affected him. Trumpf was being drafted into the military, and he didn't want to go. He was not healthy and was not even able to work the vineyards that his parents owned. He was suited to indoor work, and being a barber allowed him to earn a living without having to be outdoors.

With the draft imminent, he decided that leaving his home under the cover of darkness would be best. It would give his mother plausible deniability of her son's whereabouts, and it would save him the pain of having to say good-bye—not to mention that his mother would not have given him permission to go.

He saved up as much as he could and sold whatever he owned. He had decided to seek out his sister in New York and then make his way from there. He did not like books and could barely read. For all his conventional shortcomings, he more than compensated for it in his drive and ambition. He was willing to work hard as long as that work was not outside and without the added risk to life and limb. As such, a career in the military was out. Those two traits were exactly what the New World was looking for. The clarion call that was heard around the world was looking to fall on ears of such people as Friedrich Trumpf.

He was also interested in the country being a cowboy town in the sense that there was a lot of freedom to do a lot of things and not many laws and regulations to limit your prospects.

Friedrich did not have a plan as yet. All the knew was that he wanted to make it across the Atlantic, and then he would do whatever was necessary.

Young Trumpf was a sickly child and not able to take the constant exposure to the other sick people who were on board the ship. The communicable illnesses that many of the passengers carried on these ships made travel quite risky. The close quarters and humid environment made it worse.

It was the excitement and relief of being free from Bavaria and out on the open North Sea that kept him going. He arrived in New York in September and made his way to his sister's home. She was surprised to see him. No one knew he was coming to America—not even his mother who woke up the following morning and found that Friedrich was gone, leaving his letter on the dining table.

The push-pull in Trumpf's case was the combination of a new beginning in America and the fear of conscription in Bavaria. It was as simple as that. Much of Frederich's behavior and characteristics seem to have been passed on to his progeny—at least the males, as they resurfaced in his sons and grandson.

In the quest to understand a man, not only is it wise to ponder his history and present environment, but it is also beneficial to see the actions and motivations of the ancestors who preceded him.

As such, much research has been poured into understanding Friedrich Trump, President Trump's paternal grandfather, and also his maternal grandfather, who came from the islands beyond Scotland. Once Friedrich Trump arrived, he lived with his sister for a while, but he did not waste any time. He was broke when he landed and did not want to impose on her kindness. He set out to find work in Manhattan the morning after he announced his presence at the Schuster household in lower Manhattan.

Fortune had always been on his side. It normally took immigrants weeks if not months to find a job. He had heard about this and wanted to start early. He met a fellow Bavarian in the streets the morning he set out. His name was also Freidrich. It so happened that he owned a barber shop and offered young Trumpf a job that same day.

By the time he returned home that evening, he already had half a day's wages in his pocket, but he did not tell his sister just yet. He saved every bit of the money he earned and kept going out every morning and coming home every evening until he had saved up a large amount for himself. Only after the first month had passed did Friedrich reveal that he had found a job as an apprentice barber.

Friedrich saved every penny that he earned. He paid his sister some of his earnings in return for room and board but not a penny more than was required. It wasn't that he wasn't a good person or didn't care for his family, but he was a man with a plan.

He was determined to make the best of being in America as possible. His fortune was already looking up. In less than a month, he already had more money than he had ever had in his life.

Friedrich wasn't about to piddle his fortune away. He planned to save it and invest in whatever he could. For the moment, he just kept his head down and learned the language. Just because he didn't have any book smarts did not mean that he was unable to learn quickly. On the contrary, Friedrich, who by this point had Americanized his name to Fred, was a quick study.

Within a couple of weeks, he was conversant in the language and able to hold short conversations with his customers. Within a couple of months, he was fluent, and within the year he had all but lost his Bavarian accent.

Friedrich was not just good with his language. He also had a knack for commerce. He understood what it took to make money, and he didn't let anything, including regulations and laws, stop him.

If you are thinking this sounds a lot like the

current occupant of the White House, you wouldn't be wrong, but this is not in any way a bad thing.

He stayed with his sister the entire time he was in New York. The whole family had moved from the lower end of Manhattan to midtown because of rising prices, and they wanted to save money. Other than that, Friedrich kept working and saving at the barber shop until he was about twenty-one. By this point, he had saved almost a thousand dollars.

The purchasing power of a thousand dollars in 1891 is approximately that of $27,000 today. This was hardly a feather in his cap, but it did show a tremendous amount of restraint and focus. There is no record of Fred sending money back to his mother or giving his sister more than his share of earnings. He was focused on one thing—to find opportunity. That came in 1891.

With enough saved up, he decided to move out West. A typical trip across the country would take about five to six weeks. Fred took a train on the relatively new transcontinental railroad, and it took him a week. The cost back then for steerage sleeper fare was about $65 to get him from coast to coast. Once in California, it took another week to get up to Washington, which had just recently been granted statehood.

At this point, Fred was twenty-two years old and had been living in the United States for almost seven years. His mannerisms had changed, and he was able to fit in better. He had built himself up to the point that he could move from being a worker to a business owner.

He evaluated his prospects and resources and realized that his thousand-dollar nest egg would not go very far if he remained in New York. His best bet was to seek an opportunity for freedom and growth. With that frame of mind, he chose Washington.

One of Fred's defining characteristics was that he didn't make a move without first planning it out or thinking about it. That is not to say that he didn't take risks or that he was afraid to jump in. He didn't seem to think about the reasons he should or shouldn't do something. Instead, he thought about what he needed to do to overcome the inherent risks and obstacles.

His plan to get to Washington was to beat the rest of the people who were going there. He turned out to be right. His instincts told him that he had to provide some sort of service for those who were arriving, and with that in mind, he went to downtown Seattle and purchased a brothel. Fred had no qualms about what business he was in. He didn't consider one thing moral or another thing immoral. He was only concerned with the profit potential in something, not its moral or ethical cost.

Brothels, salons, and entertainment were a large part of later nineteenth century frontier towns. It was a fact of life and big business. Fred's investment was in a diner on the main entertainment street. He purchased it, upgraded with the money he had saved up, and served alcohol. New states did not have many rules, regulations, and laws or federal laws either.

Money may not have been the only motivation for Fred to enter the brothel business. He did enjoy the company of the ladies, and it is possible, based on rumor, that not only did he make a handsome profit on his investments when it came to food, wine, and women, but he was also able to sample the products from time to time in the name of quality control.

This was not the only time that Fred ventured into this business.

He kept the brothel for almost three years and made a tidy profit from it. When he decided it was time to sell the place and put up the entire property, including the building, fixtures, and goodwill, it was snapped up in short order.

With a pile of cash, he was able to consider the next money-making idea that would come along. For this, he considered his options and heard about the potential gold mining opportunity just outside Seattle.

The Gold Rish of California was well under way at this point, and it was not too outlandish to think that the land that stretched across the Pacific Northwest and reached south carried the same kinds of gold deposits. The Mother Lode deposits had not only enriched the pockets of many but had also enriched the imagination of thousands more. Fred knew there would be another gold rush up in Washington when more people started to hear about the small finds that were being made.

He didn't get personally or directly involved. Instead, he took his newfound wealth and moved to Monte Cristo, which was not too far from where the gold rush in Washington happened just a few years later. Something about Fred, his son, and his grandson was that they all seemed to have an uncanny ability to see into the future.

He started to understand that the way to make the most of the endeavor would be to purchase property and build something. He also realized that it would be good for him to purchase land in areas that would possibly have mining potential. He put both those ideas into action.

With the money he had saved up and the money he got from the sale of the brothel, he purchased two parcels of land. The first was in Seattle. The idea was to build a hotel/brothel, and he also bought some land near a railway station, where he wanted to build a hotel.

He purchased both. The one that he bought first ended up not being developed, but it holds the honor of being the first property of the Trump family in the United States. It was about forty acres of land outside the city limits for less than

$500.

The second plot that he purchased was right next to the railway station. This was a little more contentious than the first. He wanted this piece of land to build a brothel and a restaurant. Its location by the train tracks and the station would make it perfect for all the prospectors who would arrive by train and need a place to stay and some food to eat.

It was also the case that most of these prospectors were men. Not many families tagged along to the frontier, where the facilities were ragged, the inhabitants were rough, and the accommodations were slim.

The almost all male visitor traffic made it the best opportunity for Fred to open another brothel. There was only one problem with his plan—someone already owned that particular piece of property.

The Trumpf family, be it Fred Sr., Fred, or the highest achiever of them all, the current president, never allowed anything or anyone to stand in their way. Whether it was something tactical, legislative, or moral, it was never great enough to be an insurmountable obstacle.

Despite the plot of land belonging to someone else, Fred bribed the county clerk's office and had the property converted to his name. He built a multistory structure with a large kitchen on the ground floor, enough to cook for more than three thousand people a day, and he built a dining parlor next to it. In the upper levels, he built rooms. They were advertised as hotel rooms, and one could stay there for the night, but it was designed to be used on an hourly basis.

His instincts were right. The business did so well that the money he had loaned to build the structure was paid off in under two months. By the third month, he was free and clear of any obligations and owned the structure, but the property was now under litigation by the actual owner.

It didn't bother him that he had just yanked the property from under the nose of the actual owner. Fred continued to make money from his efforts. He worked hard, was smart, and he was prone to having a good time without taking his eyes off the businesses at hand. He was making money from the food, the alcohol, and the ladies not to mention the occasional income from those who came to the building looking for an actual room to spend the night.

After giving the legal owner much trouble, he was able to buy the land two years later for pennies on the dollar. With his nose for future events as keen as ever, Fred turned the property around and sold it for a huge profit and left town.

Within two years, it turned out that there wasn't enough gold in the area to call it a "rush." Old prospectors left, new prospectors stopped coming, and people gradually left. Even the old railroad that came into town was not upgraded or cared for and soon fell into disrepair.

All of this describes his prowess in business, but it doesn't, however, speak to his popularity, charm, and people skills. He was top shelf in these areas as well. He was one of those people who could sell ice to an Eskimo. His charm got him elected by a landslide as justice of the peace in Monte Cristo. A JP, as it is called, is similar to a magistrate's court judge. He can adjudicate misdemeanors and issue warrants if need be. S time it was a town with more gold.

Once he sold the land, he decided to move on to the next gold rush town that was taking shape. It was the Yukon gold rush, better known as the Klondike Gold Rush. Before he jumped in headfirst, though, he evaluated the prospects of making the move. A few things were not in his favor. High on that list was that he had seen how unproven claims of gold prospecting had made numerous people lose their savings. Many people actually did make money, but more lost everything. He instinctively realized that to mitigate the risk he needed to find a better way. Once he sold the boarding house in Monte Cristo, he returned to Seattle. There he met prosecutors and paid them to go up to the Yukon and stake land on his behalf. Instead of making the arduous trip himself, he had found a better way of doing things. As much as he fancied the idea of gold, panning for it with the possibility of not finding anything did not appeal to him.

Instead, he devised a plan to get involved with the speculation of land rights. He decided to purchase prospecting rights of various plots of land. In two deals, he made huge gains. In the first one, he paid less than $20 to register a claim on one plot of land. He sold half of it the next day for close to $500. On the second one, he registered it for less than $20 and sold half of it for $500 and a few weeks later sold the other half for $2,000. He did this a few times in different areas. Essentially, he put in $15 and took out $500 in the first instance after just one day. In the second instance, he put in $15 for one plot and took out $2,500 for the entire plot. These were just for the rights to mine the specific plots of land. That's $30 in investment for $3,000 in returns.

After liquidating his Monte Cristo investment, he moved back to Seattle. With the money he had saved up at this point, he purchased other property. This time he bought land that was significantly more expensive than land he had bought in the past, but he was a prudent man. He didn't want to risk all of his capital, so he borrowed a lot of money from the bank. He had good credit and was able to get the loan fairly easily.

The money was used to purchase the existing property and convert it into a restaurant. He managed the business so well that he paid off the banks in a month this time and owned the property free and clear without risking a penny of his own money.

His savings had increased tremendously, and he was making a name for himself. He was still not down with his brand of prospecting. He was bitten by the property bug and knew he could make money from it regardless of whatever rules or regulations might prevent him.

He now had the idea to make it up to the Yukon himself. He wasn't planning to prospect for gold but rather to make money from those who did go there to do the prospecting. It was always the same model of business that drove his decision-making.

The Klondike rush was totally different from Monte Cristo. First of all, Klondike had significant deposits of gold, and a greater number of prospectors went there. Aside from that, the route to get to the mining area was much harder. The Canadian government had issued advisories and regulations to protect prospectors. They required each prospector to carry a year's worth of supplies when they tracked into the Klondike. The journey was arduous and long, with no towns and supply depots along the way.

This gave rise to an opportunity. Fred realized that he could mine the miners, as he put it. He would be able to provide his trio of services, and so he set off. Along the way, by the side of the path leading to the mines, he set up tents, which were designed to provide food, rest, alcohol, and, of course, the company of ladies.

The women were transported there and so was the alcohol, but the meat for the meals was taken from the many dead horses that could not make the journey under the cold and hard conditions. It was a popular tent stop for the prospectors that soon became famous. There was no need to build structures or purchase meat, and the margin on alcohol was high. Fred made a lot of money once again.

Just around the turn of the century, Fred had found another opportunity. It was no longer enough to just run an enterprise by the side of the road in tents. He wanted to take it further. He met someone who would become a business partner—a man by the name of Ernest Levin.

Fred and Ernest got together and decided to move to British Columbia. They thought more people would be here than in the Klondike. They moved to British Columbia in 1898. They chose a town called Bennet, which was where most of the prospectors had boats built to be able to sail down the river. Here the two men built a brothel called The Arctic.

As always, it included good food, plenty to drink, gambling tables, rooms for guests, and little boxes upstairs for private parties with the ladies. Pretty soon after opening this establishment, the money started pouring in. It was the perfect choke point. Men who arrived with a year's worth of supplies and purses fresh with money—sometimes all their savings for the year they planned on prospecting—would find themselves being relieved of considerable amounts of it at The Arctic while they waited for their boats to be built.

They would spend it on the good food—this time without the horse meat—spend it on the ladies and lose what was left at the tables. Fred enjoyed his own product as well. He would have a drink now and then, enjoy the good food and also the company of the ladies, but he never went overboard.

The same could not be said for Ernest. He started enjoying the product a little too much, and it became a distraction. He was taking too much liquor from the stores, and it caught the attention of the calculative Fred.

The two began arguing and had a falling out in short order. They spent some time as unwilling partners. At around the same time, Canadian law enforcement had started scrutinizing the operations. Prostitution was not legal in Canada, and the police were not cooperating with Fred. They were not coming down hard on him, and they were not willing to be bribed either. As long as his prostitution activities and the gambling were not getting too out of hand, they were not doing much to stop him. This was a sign for Fred. Between the possibility of being clamped down by the law and the problem he was having with his partner, Fred had started to think about divesting from The Arctic.

By divesting, he managed to make the most money he had made in any endeavor up to this point. In 1901, two years after getting on the Klondike trail, he applied for his passport and made his way back to Kallstadt.

He was thirty-one years old and had spent a lot of time away from his homeland. He made his way back to New York with all his money and set sail for Bremen. This time he enjoyed better accommodations during the passage. As for The Arctic, the Canadian police finally shut it down for prostitution and gambling. Once again his luck had prevailed, and he had exited an investment at its peak.

When he arrived in Germany, he deposited the equivalent of $500,000 in a bank account and decided to stay in Germany to live the rest of his life in comfort. He began looking for opportunities to invest in and for property to purchase. What he found was an opportunity to get married.

He met a girl, a local from the village, whom his mother did not approve of. Fred, however, was insistent on marrying this physically appealing woman who had all the right qualities. Her name was Elizabeth Christ.

They married the following year. Fred had known his bride when they were children. When he was sixteen, around the time he left home, she was five years old and lived next door to them. When he returned and they bumped into each other, he found that she had blossomed, he was in his early twenties, and it was enough to want to get married.

Elizabeth Christ was born in 1880 to Phillip Christ and his wife. The family was also winegrowers, just like the Trumpfs. But, just as the Trumpfs, their income was not enough, and both her parents had to take on extra work for additional income. They were barely scraping through, and Elizabeth was no stranger to hard times. She was pretty intelligent, though, and also strong-willed.

Soon after they married, she became pregnant and boarded a vessel in Bremen to return to New York. It was Fred's idea to return, but it was hard to do for Elizabeth. When they reached New York, they found an apartment in the Bronx. At the time, the Bronx was predominantly populated with German-speaking immigrants. Elizabeth found comfort in this because her English was not as fluent as Fred's, and she didn't learn it as quickly as he did until much later. For a start, as soon as she landed, it was best to keep the family in an environment that resembled home.

Fred knew that it would be hard for Elizabeth to be away from her family, and choosing the Bronx was his way of managing the situation. Despite his best efforts, however, she became homesick. It became so severe that they had to return to Germany. By this point, they had changed their names to Fred and Elizabeth Trump. They returned to Germany, thinking they were leaving New York for the last time and would not return.

When they got to Kallstadt, they found a house and started life once again. Elizabeth was pregnant with the first child soon after. Then, his past caught up with him. The authorities had discovered that Friedrich Trumpf was a draft dodger. They knew that he had fled to America when he was supposed to sign up for the army.

To his credit, Fred tried every which way he could to get out of the situation, and he was fortunate that their punishment was to banish him from the kingdom and not something worse, such as incarceration or a court-martial. He was forced to leave the country and not return. No matter what he did, he was not able to reverse the government's decision, so he and Elizabeth had to return to New York.

They returned in 1905, found another place in the Bronx, and this time she gave birth to their second child, Fred Christ Trump. Elizabeth was a year old. Two years after that they had their third child, John George. With three children, they decided they needed a larger place and moved to Queens.

John George Trump was their last child, and he was born in 1907. He later became a distinguished professor at MIT.

Fred Sr. continued working for a little while longer and maintained a job as a hotel and restaurant manager. He was no longer interested in building and managing brothels. It would not be the right thing to do if one wanted to provide a wholesome life for his family.

The job at the hotel did not last long, however, and Fred was eager to get back to business. He reentered the business world while he was still a manager at the hotel by purchasing a seven-room, two-story building. He moved the family into one of the areas of the building and rented out the rest of it. He was able to cover the mortgage from the rental he collected from the tenants, which enabled the family to live rent free. He still had most of his assets intact and started to accumulate properties around New York.

He also opened a barbershop at 60 Wall Street. He didn't do the work, but he engaged other barbers to work and paid them a salary. His grandson later bought one of the buildings down the road at 40 Wall Street, and it had the family name emblazoned on the plaque—Trump Tower.

By the time John was born, Elizabeth had learned to speak proper English, but she always seemed to have an accent that caused her to stand out from the crowd, but she didn't mind at all. Her accent was quaint and reminded the family of their heritage.

Elizabeth was not the typical quiet lady one

might expect. She was not the usual house chores and babies kind of person. She was young, attractive, and bursting with energy. She grew to become Fred's most trusted counsel.

Over the next few years, they gradually accumulated more land. In time, he purchased vacant lots in land-strapped Manhattan. He purchased some for cash, and he acquired bank loans to execute for others. He also started buying stock in companies and accumulated wealth by being a shrewd investor.

His plan was to develop the lands that he bought. Elizabeth and Fred worked diligently at saving and looking for properties below market value. They also found properties that they could get inexpensively and then built them up and rented them out. They found that rental properties were better than properties they would buy and flip.

The key to the Trump strategy was to build cash flow instead of just looking for capital appreciation. Building for cash flow gave them cash flow today and capital appreciation tomorrow. It became the Trump strategy after that for three generations and counting.

In 1918, one of the world's greatest natural disasters occurred. Fred Sr. was forty-nine years old at that time, Elizabeth Sr. was thirty-eight, and Elizabeth Jr., Fred Jr., and John were fourteen, thirteen, and eleven respectively. The disaster killed almost 4 percent of the world's population over a period of two years between 1918 and 1920. It was the H1N1 virus, otherwise known at the time as the Spanish Flu.

Fred Senior had contracted the flu from somewhere and died less than twenty-four hours later. The family was devastated. Fred Jr., who was especially close to his father, was the worse hit of the three children, but he was also the bravest of the three. He regrouped quickly, realizing that he was the eldest man in the house and the default heir, which also meant that it was his responsibility to look after the family and build the business his father was in the midst of ramping up.

On the one hand, he had to look after his family, and on the other, he had to extend his father's legacy. The one small issue at this point, however, was that he was still a minor. As such, he and his mother started a company called Elizabeth Trump & Son. It was renamed The Trump Organization in the early 1970s by Elizabeth Trump's grandson and Donald John Trump, the forty-fifth president of the United States.

Fred Christ Trump was forced to grow up overnight and grow up he did. The entire family, on both sides of his ancestry, the Trumps and the Christs, was Lutheran to the bone. His mother, a devout Lutheran, did inculcate the lessons of the church when they were young children before her husband had passed.

For the rest of the book, we will refer to Fred Christ Trump as Fred and his father as Senior.

Fred was a smart child. Most children who lose their father at a young age are forced to mature rapidly and take on the role of protector and guardian. Fred filled this role superbly. He was not unlike his father in many ways except that he was purely American. He was born in the Bronx and attended kindergarten and grade school in America. He was turning out to be an all-American teenager and had a keen eye for business just like his father. He was just a little younger than his father when he had to grab the reins of life and make things happen instead of sitting back and let them happen.

Fred attended Richmond Hill High School in Jamaica, Queens. While he went to school, he also took classes on how to read blueprints. Then came Henry Ford and the Model T. It became apparent that the automobile was here to stay, and more and more families were buying their personal transportation in the form of cars. Now they needed somewhere to park them. This is where Fred Trump first got his break at age fifteen. He started building garages as extensions to homes while attending school. He was too young to sign checks and manage the payments, so his mother came to his aid.

Fred Trump was a hardworking young man. He never stopped working and building the business, and soon it was earning real money that his mother initially thought it wouldn't. She knew there would be some returns, but she didn't expect Fred to make as much as he did.

He found that the money he made from building garages was not going to be the be-all-end-all. He was going to save it up to do something more. His mother advised him to save as well and learn the trade and take it one step at a time.

He was in such a hurry, though, that by the time he was twenty he had built his first house by his own hand. The house was sold, and he moved on to his next project. Besides building garages, he began to do remodeling and building homes. The Trump family income increased—not just in absolute terms but in hourly terms as well. He started making more per unit of time that he put into it.

Fred was as frugal as they come. He would find ways to save pennies on everything. When he would visit construction sites to inspect the work done by the workers during the day, he would scour the grounds for nails and screws and then put them back in the bin to be used the next day.

Once his buildings were built and rented out, if tenants complained about pests, such as cockroaches and ants, instead of spending $2 per gallon (at the time) on pesticides, he would get a sample of it, take it to the chemist, ask them for the ingredients, and then make it himself. He found that it saved him $1.50 per gallon.

Fred didn't have time to enjoy his childhood. There was always a sense of responsibility toward his mother and siblings. The weight of supporting a family is heavy on any man, but it is compounded if one is still a teenager. On the one hand, he was thrilled to be making money, but he was also worried that he wouldn't make enough.

Most teenagers at fourteen or fifteen did not need to do what Fred was doing, and if paternal guardianship was unexpectedly interrupted, most turned to the surviving parent or extended family for survival. In Fred's case, it was reversed. He wasn't asked to or compelled to take on the burden—it was something that he just wanted to do and felt deeply that it was his responsibility.

Chapter 2 The Rising

A personal characteristic that repeatedly shows up in the Trump family line is that they have always reached for a place higher than where they presently stood.

It was more than ambition, which is a short-term spurt of motivation compared with this quality that the Trumps seem to display. They want something more than what they have at the time. This trait is not common even among those who eventually make it to the top. Whether it is someone like Lincoln who redefined the presidency or men like Vanderbilt who altered the window of discourse, men from the Trump clan are not easily found, and thus, not easily defined.

It's easy to define men who fall into typical categories. It's easy to identify such traits as valor and talk about the concept of bravery because most people are made familiar with these characteristics early in life. But when it comes to Trump, it is hard to define and put into context because the Trumps—not just the men but also the Trump women these men chose to marry—instinctively had the characteristic that has catapulted them to ever-higher levels of success and achievement. From Johannes Trump and his vineyard to Frederich Trump and his brothels to Fred C for his low-cost development of houses, each man has climbed onto the shoulders of his father and reached even higher.

The essence of that drive is what this biography attempts to uncover. Revealing that essence allows the actions of the man to be of benefit to one's own inspiration and eventual achievements in the world.

Each man can either use the man who came before him as a stepping stone or as a dead weight. One allows him to ascend, while the other compels him to sink. Enough ink has been spilled on the calamities and contemptuous nature of the forty-fifth president. That does not serve any of us any good, but there are threads of success and achievement that we can all pull on and learn from, and that is the key to any biography, especially this one.

To see President Trump's rise from rich child to president is most astounding because it is something that most conventional thinking people will not be able to guess or fathom. That is one of the many reasons why none of the polls could predict that he would win over the favorite in the race.

Put aside all issues of collusion (there is no legal standard or definition of the term) or the possibility of a conspiracy to win an election. In one of that has any actual basis in reality. Just as Clinton's impeachment had no bearing on his job as Chief Executive, nothing that has been leveled in terms of accusations against President Trump really makes any sense and has anything to do with his executive responsibilities as Chief Executive. As for his tax returns, he doesn't need to provide them. It is not a requirement, and if it were it would be codified as law somewhere. It is not. If someone wants to publicize their tax returns, that's up to them, but they shouldn't need to. One's tax returns do not tell anyone their ability to do the job of representing the people.

This book is not intent on litigating any of the political matters for the purpose of casting shade on the president or his enemies. The dive into politics that we will make as we turn the page is more to show his temerity and tenacity rather than his ideas.

If you really think about it, President Trump has been a Democrat all his life. He may not have voted, but he certainly supported Democrats more than he supported Republicans. But he was smart. He didn't need to back any particular chore, and he didn't have to. That's exactly who you want as president. As president, you're the representative of all people, not just those who share your ideology. That is hard to do if you have an ideology. Trump doesn't have one. That's exactly who you want in the White House.

As for Fred Jr., by the time he was twenty-one, his business was moving ahead in full swing. He had set his sights on the construction industry, and it fit his temperament and skill set perfectly.

He had made use of the opportunities that came about with the development of the automobile and built hundreds of garages and porches for his neighbors in Queens and beyond. He then went into building homes in the area and was able to provide custom-built homes at relatively cheap prices and had a profitable business.

He and his mother knew about Fred Sr.'s plans to develop land, and this was in the back of Junior's mind, but time had not presented the opportunity just yet. For now, he was focused on the construction aspect of it.

Then came the opportunity in the form of Roosevelt's homeownership programs and the Housing Authority. Fred recognized that this was the time for him to strike. He decided to buy land, which he could not easily afford or have enough credit to purchase. He did so in such areas as Queens and as far away as Maryland. It is a common misconception that the Trumps only developed land in New York. The truth is that they were in areas outside the five boroughs as well.

Once he bought the land, he started to put up simple, no-frills, high-density apartments that he would rent out. This was an amazing business model that transformed the neighborhood and the balance in his (and his mother's) bank account. These homes turned out to be quite successful.

The primary model of business at the start was to put a down payment on the purchase of the land, which was not very much in lower-income neighborhoods. It was easily affordable by then cash-rich Fred. This was after a decade of building garages and modest homes.

Once he purchased the land, he would take on another load for the construction and build a tower of simple brick buildings. One can still find a large number of these buildings in the lower-income neighborhoods, such as Bensonhurst, Coney Island, and Sheepshead Bay.

One could say he was the pioneer in budget businesses. His idea was never to sell expensive properties to rich people. There was not much profit in that in those days. It would be easy to predict that if he did the same business in the late twentieth century when overpriced housing was common that he may have considered doing it, but it just was not his character to flash money and extract profit from low-volume, high-margin endeavors.

You could tell that Fred was a budget business kind of person because he was the original inventory of the supermarket. Before Fred, everyone went to the corner grocery store and had store owners and their staff get products for you from behind the counter. Then came Fred's grocery store where the advertisement promised lower prices in return for customers getting their own things off the shelf. Fred determined that the fewer people he could hire, the less he could charge customers, and the less he could charge customers, the more customers he would get.

This is the model of the grocery store today. In fact, it is getting so far ahead of itself that such companies as Amazon are now even doing away with the cashier and making that automated. All that came from the model that Fred Trump first created. He built a number of these self-service grocery stores and eventually sold them to the King Kullen chain for a very large profit. King Kullen was recently in talks to be sold to Shop & Save.

It was always about cutting costs and selling cheap. He didn't need to be altruistic or feel that he had to do it so that the customer could benefit. There was nothing magnanimous about it. Fred was not looking to raise the middle-income or the lower-income groups. He was pragmatic. He just pursued a market that he recognized.

He was accused of many things, one of which was that he was racist and didn't want to rent to a certain quarter of society. He may have been racist, or he may just have been someone who wanted to make money. He didn't want the problem of not being able to collect the rent that he was owed, and a simple mind will tell you that if you rented to a certain segment of society the chances of getting your rent check on the day it is supposed to arrive is lower. Of course, in the eyes of the law, that is racist and goes against equality, but that is not how he saw it.

There is no intention to apologize for Fred here, but there is also no intention to follow along with the crowds of people who accused him of racism and tarnish his reputation. The point is that Fred was in it to make money. He didn't spend that money lavishly, and he didn't boast about his money.

The only thing that he ever spent money on, perhaps even splurging a little, was his Cadillac. He really liked dark blue Cadillacs with his FCT vanity plate, and he would always keep it shiny. He would religiously trade in the car for a new one every three years and drive it himself wherever he went. That was the extent of his extravagance. Otherwise, he saved every penny and spent it on the next project.

Fred Trump believed in loans but only when he could maximize the return on his investment. He would not accept or draw on a loan that reduced his profit by even a penny. It was never about shunting the risk to the banker. He never intended to not pay the banker either.

Just like his father and grandfather before him, Fred Trump always acted with integrity and dignity. He paid every loan and didn't borrow when he could not pay it back. When he first started building single-family homes, he bought the plot of land, built the home, and then sold it for just under $4,000. He made good margins on these buildings and managed to finish them quickly. The designs were simple but sturdy. He wanted to sell them cheap, but he was not going to undercut the sturdiness or the safety of the building.

They were simple red brick, plasterboard buildings. They were not fancy, but they were made to be widely affordable. By the time Fred had started building these houses, he had been putting John, his younger brother, through school. John first went to Brooklyn Polytechnic Institute. He tried architecture and found that he had a knack for it. He wanted to pitch in and help his brother and started designing homes. These were the homes that were first built by Fred. When the time came to sell it, John was hesitant. He saw it more as an engineering work of art and was reluctant to part with it. Ever the businessman, however, Fred was not attached to it in any way. He wanted to sell the property and move on to the next one.

In the end, John relented and realized that he didn't have the same frame of mind as his older brother. So he went back to school, changed his major to electrical engineering, and didn't look back. Fred had the building gene in the family. From Brooklyn, John went on to Columbia to pursue his Masters in electrical engineering and then to the Massachusetts Institute of Technology to complete his doctorate. He then became a professor of engineering at MIT.

John owed much of his financial backing and ascent through the ranks of expensive schools to his brother's generosity, but it was not Fred's generosity that financed his little brother's academic rise. It was Fred's sense of responsibility. It was about Fred stepping into his father's shoes soon after he died.

There was a bond between Fred and his father. Fred knew his father to be a man of great accomplishment and took him to be a powerful role model. Snatched away at a young age, Fred saw it as a role he was meant to fill and so raised the other two children in a way he believed his father would have. There was nothing magnanimous about it. It was filial in nature and responsible in conduct. It is also the reason we need to see Fred as a man before his time. He became who he was not because of his character but because of the surroundings he was thrust into by the Spanish Flu epidemic.

Fred Christ (pronounced krist) Trump went on to build massive apartment buildings, but there is one twist that one needs to understand. It is easy to think that he built big buildings because of his fascination with size, but that was not it. Fred was a calculating man and wanted to optimize everything he had. He built the buildings to maximize utility on one plot of land using the technology available to him at that time. If he could have built an infinitely tall building that would last for a long time and be filled up to the last apartment, he would have. Instead, he built what he could given the building technology and tools of the time. He chose red brick buildings not for style but for sturdiness. He cared about sturdiness because of one thing—he wasn't selling those buildings. He was renting out the apartments.

The key to remember is that he didn't think of doing this based on a whim. He chose to build these buildings that you still see today in various parts of New York because of necessity and opportunity. He wanted the cash flow of rental so that when he borrowed the money to build the apartments the rental he collected repaid the loan. He did this on an accelerated fashion.

The more rental he collected, the faster he was able to repay the loan. The faster he repaid the loan, the less interest he would end up paying. It was all about necessity. This is the main reason why he didn't want to rent to anyone he thought might pay their rental later than normal or not at all. It is also why they never told anyone he was German or, more accurately, Bavarian.

He wanted those buildings completely occupied, and to do that he needed to rent to a large number of people, many of them of the Jewish faith. If he had told them he was German, it would have been a bit of a problem. He was not lying to ensnare them; he was lying to conceal what he couldn't control. He couldn't control the negative view others had of Germans in the '30s. He himself was not racist. If anything, he knew what it felt like to be discriminated against. His parents, Fred and Elizabeth, were born in Bavaria, not Hitler's Germany—but the Bavarian and German name had been mixed up with the

Nazi activities of a man he had no relationship with. He also saw the kind of headache that Henry Ford was getting for sympathizing with some of the Nazi philosophy.

That desire to not be associated with the Germans led the change in the narrative of the Trump family. They were from that point on to be known as a family that emigrated from Sweden. This was not a random choice. He didn't just pick a country to fake his origins. He chose one based on a homophone of his origin. His parents came to from Kallstadt, Bavaria, but he said they came from Karlstad, Sweden. Pretty smart.

That worked well, and no one doubted him. Besides, Fred had no trace of any German accent. He seemed to be entirely American. He was intelligent, full of energy, and handsome and had been described as a man who could have been a successful movie star. Fred was indeed charismatic. Even when his hair was gray, he was a good-looking man and charming as well. He could speak with authority and charm, making the men who worked for him pay attention. No one around him would ever disobey one of his commands because they had full confidence that Fred knew what he was talking about.

When he decided to expand out of New York, he set his sights on the vicinity of Chester, Pennsylvania, where the Navy had a yard in nearby Philadelphia. In pursuit of this market, he built homes for the military and returning veterans.

One of his competitors, a Mr. LeFrak, builder of Lefrak city, also built low- and medium-cost apartments, was highly appreciative of his contemporary. The diligence that Fred showed during his time as one of the country's most prolific builders is a testament to his achievements. When a competitor can praise you, you know you have made a difference in the world.

In the end, Fred built almost fifty thousand apartments, mostly on the East Coast. All the time he was building and becoming wealthy, which was not common in those days, he kept his head down, provided for his mother and siblings, and did his best to keep his costs low.

Then he met a Mary Anne MacLeod, who had just arrived in New York from the upper islands of Scotland. She was working in the city as a maid. She was currently staying with her two sisters who had also emigrated from the upper islands of Scotland. She was the youngest of ten children of Mary and Malcolm MacLeod.

Life was simple in the islands. Her family was primarily involved in the fishing trade, and her father worked at the school that Mary Anne and her siblings attended. She did learn to speak English, but it was not her first language, which was Gaelic, and those who speak Gaelic from birth are not able to speak English without an interesting accent that is sweet and captivating. Mary Anne met Fred at a dance that she had been brought to by her two sisters, who had emigrated to the United States before she did and knew their way around the social stage better then she did.

He was particularly attracted to the sound of her voice. She was noticeably shorter than the dapper and towering Fred Trump, but they made a very handsome couple. They were one of those couples that you just enjoy watching as they got along and dated. It was the 1930s now, the economy was on an upswing, and dating was more in fashion than any other previous generation. Fred and Mary Trump looked like the Ronald and Nancy Reagan of the East Coast.

Mary was an economic migrant, which was the classification of the U.S. Immigration Department at the time. An economic migrant is a category for emigrants that come over because conditions in one's country are so bad that they would not be able to get work or survive. Upon entry, she declared that she was coming to America and planned on seeking citizenship. She was given a temporary visa and accepted. She had only $50 when she landed in New York.

After dating for some time, Mary Anne returned to Scotland to inform her parents that she was getting married, and they gave her their permission. She returned to the United States under a reentry permit and then married Fred Trump on January 11, 1936.

The marriage produced five children: Mary Ann who was born in 1937, followed by Frederich Trump in 1938. Their third child was Elizabeth in 1942, followed by Donald in 1946, and Robert in 1948. The last pregnancy had some complications that resulted in her not being able to conceive and bring a child to term. Mary Tump stayed home except to help a little with Fred's business. While he drove his dark blue Cadillac around town, she was busy navigating her rose-colored Rolls-Royce.

While Fred was a no-nonsense kind of guy, Mary Anne had grown up seeing the wealthy class treating poor folk, like her family, poorly. The MacLeods lived on the coast and were so near the water that during high tide the road out front would turn to mud. It was not easy to live under those conditions, as the streets would smell like a sewer, and families in the area would need to wear boots to get from one place to the next; otherwise, they would be knee-deep in the muck that would pile up along the streets.

The families that lived there had long since given up on cleaning up after the tide and learned to live with the stench. They may have lived in squalor, but they were good people. They went to church every Sunday, which back then was an all-day affair. It was also brutal. The path they had to take to town where the church was located passed through terrain that would be easily submerged under water during high tide, and members of some of the families often drowned when making their way to church. Yet, no one missed church unless there was an accident.

On their way, they passed houses that were the crème de la crème of the town. These were where the well-heeled English had come to live. They never treated the locals well, but they were forgiven.

As if the poverty weren't catastrophic enough, World War I came, and the families of the poor sent their sons off to fight in a war far away from where they lived. It was a small town, and all the men they could afford were enough to fit a number of ships. After being whittled down by the war itself, only enough men to fit one ship returned. That ship constituted the bulk of the men who would go on to be the next generation of Lewis Island. That ship ran aground within sight of shore and sunk, taking all the men with it.

That event was the last straw for many of the young women of Lewis Island. Slowly they started emigrating to the United States, most of them as maids. Out of the ten children that made up the MacLeod family, nine set sail at different times for America. Only one stayed to look after the parents. Mary Anne MacLeod returned every year bearing gifts for her family in Scotland for as long as her parents were alive.

The poor on the island were not respected. They were made to feel the poverty in terms of the indignation of the rich folk who arrived from the south. They came to the island to get away from the crowded capital and had bought their wealth with them. That wealth created a great disparity between the rich and the locals who were having trouble just getting by from one day to the next. Even though they fished for a living, they didn't have much to eat, but they did as well as they could. The living conditions in which they survived were worse.

Mary Anne hated feeling poor and loved seeing the trappings of the rich that she was forced to endure every Sunday, but endure she did. Not only did she learn to put up with it, but she also wanted it more than anything else in the world. She had no idea how she would get it, but she just knew that she was tired of living a life where mud and waste were on the streets in front of her house. Mary Anne MacLeod left the Isle of Lewis and sailed to America aboard the *SS Transylvania*.

We all get what we really wish for, and the Trumps were no different. Fred Trump wished to raise his family in his father's stead, and he did. Mary Anne wished for riches and found Fred—when he was still a normal man.

It wasn't until after they wed that the businesses started to flourish. Mary Anne was in charge of collecting the coins from all the washers and dryers that were in all the buildings that the Trumps owned. She would make the rounds in her Rolls-Royce. It was unmistakable when it came around. The vanity plate read MMT. Fred's was FCT, and President Trump's to this day is DJT. For Mary Anne, the new life she found in America was all that she prayed for and all that she wanted. She wanted to alter the trajectory of her life and live in a mansion, such as one of those she saw en route to church every Sunday. What she got was even better. She got her riches, her fur coats and Rolls-Royce, and she found a man who loved her to the ends of the earth.

The wealth she found and the man she married were a blessing from heaven. If she had struck the lottery and got her money that way, things would have been bad because she really didn't know how to handle the freedom and the luxury that came with that wealth. But the husband she found was a and of stable and coherent thought. He had no inclination to waste his money in frivolous and unproductive ways.

There was a significant difference in the kind of humble background that Fred and Mary came from. Fred had worked himself out of his beginnings with the help of his father's savings and his mother's prudence. Mary had fallen into it without having to work for it, but she had Fred there to guide her.

Chapter 3 The Window

The Overton Window is a framework that exists in modern discourse, and it is a metric and measure of the quantitative and qualitative extent of the discourse. To understand the Trump Effect, as we will look at in the next chapter, it only makes sense that we understand the Overton Window and how it has applied to everyone except Trump.

To really understand Trump, we need to look at the gravitational effects that happen all around him and far away from him. He is a powerful force in our century, and anyone who neglects this fact does so at their own peril. Once you understand the Overton Window and how to apply it to the present discourse—whatever that is—then you can start to see how that applies to others and maybe understand why it does not apply to our subject at hand.

The Overton Window can be thought of as the acceptable range of discourse. If you take the infinite possibilities of topics of conversation, the Overton Window is the range within that spectrum that is acceptable to the widest audience possible. The best way to explain it is to use President Trump as the quintessential example of the concept.

We can divide everyone into two groups. At any point in time, we can make a binary division and divide all people into this format of a framework. One group agrees, and the other disagrees. The reasons for their agreement or disagreement are not the issue.

For instance, take the issue of euthanasia. At any given point in time, some people will agree with it and others disagree. In those binary perspectives, there would be those who sit on the far end of the spectrum who agree with it in absolute terms without equivocation and those who disagree with it without exception. The two extremes will find that they have no common ground if they were forced to sit down and talk about the matter. They would be so diametrically opposed to each other's perspective and understanding that the point one party brings up would almost feel insulting and inappropriate.

But for those who have a slightly less rigid view of their position, they would be someone in the inner spectrum or plane of the conversation, and as you move close to the center of mass of this spectrum you find that the opponents of the topics have a certain area that they could sit down and talk about. It is a place where a range of the opposition's views are unacceptable but do not prevent further discussion.

That space on the spectrum is the Overton Window—for that one topic—but this is just for conversation's sake. The Overton Window is not about one topic. It is about more than that. It is about a range of topics that make up a particular society. Imagine the single topic of euthanasia. Now imagine a range of topics that are either linked to it or not and you stitch them together. For instance, consider such subjects as abortion, euthanasia, and bigamy. You start putting these topics on top of each other and find that they create a range of conversation that is acceptable and areas that are unacceptable.

If you line up each layer where the conversation is acceptable, what you find if you think about this visually is a rectangle of acceptability. Everything inside the window is acceptable, and everything outside is irreconcilable and unacceptable. If you then keep your conversation and your views within that window, you will find that you have a large audience that will agree with you.

But then some people come along who not only know how to pick out that area of commonality but also how to move it. President Trump is just such a person. This requires a significant amount of skill and inherent ability that most people who rely on cerebral cognition are unable to figure out and land up underestimating the person with this skill.

A very telling incident in the 2016 election that no one could understand is how he won the election against all odds. The key to understanding Trump is understanding why he won.

Let's forget Russia and all the other issues that may have tipped the balance. The reason why many of these externalities have been brought into the fold is that the intelligent among us can't bring themselves to see what is apparent to the rest of us. It should remind you of the time that the scientists (the intelligent ones among us) were absolutely certain that space was a void. As proof, they offered that nothing could be detected are seen and as such, there is nothing there. Now they tell us that there is something called Black Matter.

It is like what happened on election night. The intelligent among us said that their polls predicted that Trump would lose. Instead, he won. It is not because of the Russians or the Asians or the Arabs. No one put Mr. Trump in office other than those who went out to vote for him.

That's the beauty of democracy and the beauty of the Electoral College. When the EC was put into place by the founders, they were adamant about one thing. They didn't want popularity to rule the day. They went out of their way to make sure this didn't happen. The election turned out exactly the way it should have.

We live in a world that has come to rely on logic and reasoning. That ability has helped us navigate the age of enlightenment and the age of data, but there is more. There are things that can't be quantified in data that we can easily understand or communicate. There are two kinds of people when it comes to this subject: (1) those who totally reject all possibility of something that is outside their purview and (2) those who believe that there is something beyond what they can rationalize. Those people who voted for Trump are the kind of people that looked at him and said, "There is a man that has something more." These are the same people that don't fall into the typical net that pollsters use. If they can't be polled, does that mean they don't count? The election of 2016 has taught us that we can't just rely on the polls that have been dipping the measuring stick into the common pool.

Think about that for a minute. A great many people live a lifestyle that is beyond the sample set of most pollsters. Almost every single one of those folks voted for Trump. The other side did not anticipate the size of that pool, and while the final vote count was close, it was a far cry from what they thought it would be. The Clinton campaign thought they would beat the Trump campaign by a mile and instead they lost.

Why was this not predictable? Even the almost-always-accurate pollsters, such as Nate Silver, did not see the Trump win. All this goes to the point of understanding Trump himself. There is no poll or analyst that can beat his own instinct. When he said that he could shoot someone in the middle of Fifth Avenue and it wouldn't affect his supporters, he wasn't bragging and boasting. He was right.

Trump has the gift to give people exactly what they want, and the more they appreciate him for it, the more he gives them what they want. That is the symbiotic relationship between him and those who support him. The quest in this book is to find out how he managed to get that way. The question is how did he manage to drag the Overton Window so far to the point that was once unacceptable and make it what it is today. To be sure, he has not made it acceptable, but he has made people not care.

For that, we need to look at the dynamic between him and the two forces that drove his life during his youth. There is no doubt that Trump is very smart, but he is not book smart. His intelligence is more of a universal and intuitive intelligence. One does not need to quote Shakespeare or know Socrates to be able to represent the majority in this country.

The root of Trump's unique ability goes back to his experiences during childhood and the influence his father and mother had on him. To a lesser degree, it was also the influence the generation and the power of wealth had on him. Besides that, it was as much as what he had that influenced him to what he didn't have.

In the second half of this book, we will look at the influences of this intelligent and good-looking man who had everything in the world and wanted more. His definition of more was influenced by his mother and his own assumptions of what more meant. Just because there isn't a low-key sense in any part of him does not mean that one must discount the influence his father had on him. Fred Jr. had just about the same influence on him as Fred Sr. had on Junior.

Chapter 4 The Game

Once again a binary example is the simplest way to frame everything and everyone at the start. From there we can make subtle, surgical changes to tweak the specifics, but for the start, the binary approach is best. There are two kinds of people and two kinds of situations. You can place them in mental quadrants if you like, but you don't have to. It's called the Game Matrix.

There are two kinds of games. There is the finite game and the infinite game. If you can reduce everything in the universe into a game, then what you see is that you need both to make the world go around—finite and infinite activities.

The first kind of person is the one that is suited for the infinite game, and the second kind of person is the kind that is suited to the finite game. To make it simple, we assume that there is no player on the planet who can oscillate between one and the other.

What does all this mean? If you look at the full range of objectives to be reached and the activities that elevate a person from one accomplishment to the next, what you find is that you can categorize everything into short or long horizons. Things that are best completed over the long term are best not viewed as short-term goals. In the same way, people who are naturally short-term goals kind of people do poorly when attempting projects that take an extended horizon to accomplish.

This is the essence of the Game Matrix. The finite game refers to objectives and accomplishments that are typically driven by short-term gains and bite-sized challenges. Quarterly goals and targets are considered finite games. Even annual goals can be considered finite games, but building a legacy over the long term is an Infinite Game. Building Space X was the result of an Infinite Game mentality by Elon Musk. On the other hand, dealing with Washington news cycles that can change three times a day requires a deft hand in playing the finite game.

Which is better? Is it better to be an infinite player or a finite one? Unfortunately, that is not the right question. There are actually two questions you have to answer. The right one is about which player you are. Are you a finite player or an infinite player? Once you know which one you are, then you need to ask the second question: Which game are you playing— the finite game or the infinite game?

When an infinite player plays an infinite game, he wins. When a finite player plays a finite game, he wins. However, if a finite player plays an infinite game, he loses. The same goes for the infinite player playing a finite game.

Many people tend to ask what happens when two people play against each other. The answer is that this is not that sort of game. It is not a game where you compete with someone. This is about the person and his opportunities, the person and his environment. Winning and losing is not about vanquishing the opponent. It is about conquering oneself and choosing the game that best suits who you are at any given point in time.

A finite game is one where the player plays for the profit of today and lets go of whatever may profit him tomorrow. The Infinite Game is the opposite. He plays for the long-term profit at the expense of a quick and small return today.

What is President Trump, and which game is he playing? Is he the kind of man who plays for today so that he can win now, or is he the kind of person that plays for the long-term gain? The answer is obvious. He always plays for the immediate take. His father, on the other hand, was a man who played for the long-term gain—an Infinite Player. That's the reason why he doesn't look to sell the buildings he constructs to make a one-off profit now but instead rents them out and collects the income in perpetuity.

How can they both be winners? In the end, the answer is that the man who makes it is not the man who is an infinite player or the man who is a finite player. The key to winning is to match the man with the game. If the man is an infinite player, then the man should play the infinite game. If the man is a finite player, then he should play the finite game. In the case of Trump, he is a finite player, and he has always played the finite game. Whenever he has tried to play the infinite game, he has failed. You can think about Trump University and Trump Airlines to name just two. Just because a Finite Player fails at the Infinite Game doesn't mean that he is inadequate or incompetent.

The presidency is a finite game. Many people mistakenly think that it is an Infinite Game. They are confusing the country with the presidency when they do that. The country and the presidency are not the same. The country is an infinite resource and proposition, but the man at the helm has to be a Finite Player if he is to play it in a democratic setting.

If, on the other hand, he were to be a dictator, then that would parallel the country in the finite and infinite model unless that country is built on the democratic model. To make it a dictatorship, Trump would have to be an infinite player, which he has repeatedly proven that he is not. Trump would excel at being president if given the time and the space to put the policies he envisions into action. If there is any reason he fails, it would be from all the distractions that he is faced with by the opposition.

Trump is successful at making land deals because they have short-term horizons. He is successful as a politician because he only needs to go from one poll to the next. His path to the presidency has been one that has been a series of short-term gains that have eventually added up.

With the Game Matrix in mind, it is now a lot easier to layer the Overton Window that we looked at before. If you recall, the Overton

Window is the range of acceptable positions, policies, or actions that a group is willing to accept. In the case of any national politician, that group will be the constituents that vote for him. In the case of a statewide politician, it would be the state's constituents.

You can then take this one step further, as Kellyanne Conway did. You can look at the constituents in any number of ways. Most national campaigns look at a broad cross-section of voters and get an idea of what the choice would be like. For any normal candidate, that would work fine, but for a change agent such as Donald Trump, it doesn't work at all. That is why conventional wisdom failed in the last election.

A person who is a Finite Player and has the ability to shift the Overton Window drastically is the purest definition of a change agent. There are seven aspects of every analysis that need to be specified to be able to consider someone a change agent.

• Whether or not the person is a Finite Player

• Whether or not the person is able to move the Overton Window

• Whether or not the person has a clear vision

• Whether or not the leader has a relationship with the stakeholders based on trust

• Whether or not the person is able to ask tough questions

• Whether or not the person has the knowledge to lead by example

• Whether or not the person is able to ask the right questions

If you take these seven aspects and apply them to Donald Trump, what you find is that he has all the characteristics that make him a powerful change agent.

You could see it right from the start. The moment he stood at the steps of the Capitol and gave his Inaugural Address anyone listening closely would know right away that he was an agent of change.

In that respect, he has kept to his word. The moment he set foot in the oval office on the afternoon of January 20, 2017, he instantly altered the face of American politics and government.

Through most of his first term in office, he has shown that he has been a change agent in the way he has revitalized the military, abolished regulation that impedes growth, altered trade deals, and overseen the highest stock market in the history of the country not to mention the lowest unemployment rate.

As we look the rest of his achievements and actions, it is best to keep this framework of the consummate change agent and see the way he uses his skills to his advantage.

84

Chapter 5 The Beginning

Donald John Trump was born June 14, 1946, in Jamaica Hospital, Queens. He was the first among his siblings to read, write, and walk. He was a quick learner by all accounts, and he was able to show his intelligence in a number of ways. Not only was he intelligent beyond his time, but he also knew it. Being aware of his own intelligence complicated matters, as it inspired arrogance.

By the time he was five, his ability to read and write had astounded even his parents. In the 1940s, not many people were aware of how to assess characteristics of child prodigies, and so they probably never thought of testing little Donald. If they did test him, there is a good chance they would have been able to harness his potential better.

All his life he could pick up on things faster than most people his age and could remember them longer than most adults. He was good at simple math by the time he was four and had shown uncharacteristic independence at an early age. As he grew older, his math skills and people skills grew at a faster pace.

Even as a toddler, he had a keen sense of observation. The object of his observation was initially his father, but he also showed affinity and affection for his mother. He observed what she did, where she went, and how she dressed. Her flamboyance appealed to him. His sense of worth was defined by the level of attention she directed toward him from an early age, and he began to seek her approval more than he sought his father's. As for his father's traits and character, what he observed blunted his arrogance. He felt early on that his father's intellect and ability to succeed were phenomenal, which was something he wanted to emulate.

There is no doubt that he had been born with a silver spoon in his mouth. Only forty years and two generations before, the Trumps were still the Trumpfs and working hard, braving frontier obstacles to build their fortune.

His independent streak got him into trouble. He was smart but not wise enough to know his limits. He really made a nuisance of himself to his parents and siblings. To get him out of the house, he was enrolled in grade school as soon as possible. The problem with doing that, however, especially for the above-average child, is that they quickly became bored with the curriculum and then were a nuisance for the slower students.

As ambitious as his mother was, she was parochial in her academics. English was not even her first language, but she managed to pull through. She had a heavy accent and found it hard to keep up with his curiosity. The more he asked and inquired, the more she moved away from him until she soon found all the excuses one could find to stay as far away from Donald as she could.

A five-year-old is not going to understand that kind of rejection or shortcoming. He wouldn't see his mother as inadequate even if she didn't know all the answers. A five-year-old wouldn't see that his mother felt bad that she didn't know the things he was asking about, and, most certainly, a five-year-old wouldn't even think that someone would rather be somewhere else far away from their little one. It is not how any five-year-old thinks.

But that is exactly what Mary Anne MacLeod Trump did. She stayed away from her son and allowed the maid to raise, teach, and care for him. The maid was also from a Scottish village and had the same heavy accent as Mary Anne. Even under the guidance of someone other than his mother, he grew up intelligently. This was both good and bad. On one end, she skipped out on his need for affection and a companion. On the other, she left a vacuum that resulted in his outlook of women in general, but none of this was intentional. She had no idea what she was doing or the psychological mold she was creating in the process. As far as she was concerned, he was better off without her nurturing. The more he tried to draw close to her, the more she distanced herself until it came to a point that he had to act out and act up to get her attention.

In most cases, boys act out to get their father's attention but not in this case. He had dual roles as a child. He wanted to stay under the radar regarding his strict father, and he wanted to be only a blip on the radar for his mother. He didn't succeed at both. In the process, he developed a highly tuned sense of independence that worked for him effectively but didn't work out for those who depended on him for emotional support.

As busy as his father was, he still made time to keep track of Donald's development. No matter how much his father was proud of his son, however, Donald didn't think that he could live up to his father's success. He was quoted later in life as saying that he was glad his father built and conquered the outer boroughs of New York so that Donald could be left to conquer Manhattan, which always had a special allure for him. It was the jewel in the New York crown. It was the glitzy and upscale balance to the laidback and homegrown outer boroughs.

With his perspective of Manhattan and his inherent desire to attract his mother's attention, Donald started heading into Manhattan by himself and eventually getting caught up with some unsavory sorts. All this happened when he was still a pubescent twelve-year-old.

That combination of preteen angst and bursting desire to prove bravado could arguably result in a situation where a person does brash things to attract attention but never really reaches as far as their potential could take them. This was Donald at twelve, but his escapades landed him in danger and trouble. He got mixed up with switchblade gangs and was trying his hand at some typical ruffian stuff before he was found out, and his father put an end to it.

It was tough growing up in Donald Trump's shoes. He wanted to express himself and all that he was capable of, which was considerable. He felt he was smart, but he also felt that he was not getting the feedback that would confirm what he felt about himself. This created another problem. The more he tried to do better, the less it seemed he was getting positive feedback. So, the more he tried, that negative loop created a situation where he needed constant feedback to be able to dictate his next move. He found that he could get the adulation of the world outside in two ways. One was by taking charge of the narrative. The other was to be so far over the top that those around him would have no choice but to give him the feedback he needed.

Trump was always hunting for the right balance between the rules that his father put down and the freedom to do what he wanted. It was hard to walk that line just as it is with any child that age. It becomes all the more acute when the person being constrained by rules has a free spirit and a desire to reach for the stars.

His youth was defined by his free spirit. He wanted to explore and investigate, but he was made to do the opposite. Fred had high hopes for him but not because he was smart and his other children weren't. All of Fred's children showed above-normal levels of intelligence. President Trump is not kidding when he says that he is smart or has a big brain.

What most people laugh away is because one does not speak about oneself in polite company that way, but that is not who Trump is speaking to when he says such things as "I have a big brain." He is speaking to a component of his base—the people who support him for what they think he can do for them.

In this respect, Trump is like his father—being able to sell ice to an Eskimo. That ability is the result of a combination of charm and wit. Both Trumps have that in abundance. When you combine a free spirit with higher-than-average eloquence, the result is very interesting.

Trump's eloquence is not about sophisticated grammar and Shakespearean language. His brand of sophisticated eloquence is in being able to say exactly what the person wants to hear. When a commentator mocks him for what he says, that commentator does not realize that Trump can speak in the most refined manner possible, but he is speaking to a certain crowd and speaks in a way that relates to that crowd. Observe the next time he is speaking in front of a crowd or to the cameras. His language is basic, his sentence structure is in bullets, and his hands gesticulate to keep their attention. He is a master communicator and literally takes control of the space between him and his audience. His opponents, on the other hand, be it his fellow Republicans during the debates or Clinton in the presidential debates, were speaking at a level so complicated for mass distribution that there was nothing they could do to move the needle.

He won because he communicated perfectly to the crowd that responded well to his simple talk. When you hear him speak in private, he doesn't speak that way. His communication skills came from his father. When his father was a developer and builder, he would take great pains and go to great lengths to know the person he was talking to and prepare accordingly. A salesman once came to visit Fred Trump, and he was not anybody most people would consider to be important. As soon as he walked into the office, Fred got up, reached out to him, entered his personal space, and shook his hand. "Hi, I am Fred," he said. At this time, Fred was already a wealthy and established developer.

They started talking, and Fred spoke at great lengths about baseball. When he was leaving, the man commented to Fred's assistant that he had no idea that the great developer was such a fan of baseball. The assistant responded that he wasn't.

The point is that Fred went to great lengths to speak the language and the topic that was important to the man he was talking to. In return, that man became a lifelong loyalist to Fred and went on to be a powerful salesman for him.

On a separate occasion, Fred was walking into one of his buildings and encountered one of the caretakers who was polishing the floor. As Fred passed by, he said, "That's the best shine I've seen." He didn't stop and just kept going, but the assistant behind him saw the transformation in the man polishing the floor. He doubled his efforts.

Trump learned this from a young age. He learned to communicate in ways that most people, even politicians today, do not know how to do. In seventy years, he has built the innate ability to know what to say and what would create loyalty in a person. The words he uses, the fears he speaks of, the colors he chooses, the brand he associates with, and even the women he dates are all driven by how others see it and how they will feel about him when he does it.

That makes him the best public official because he knows what people want. His ability to become close to a person is also the reason why all the people who at one time despised him suddenly fell in love with him. Take his personal counselor, Kellyanne Conway, as an example. Before signing up with team Trump, she was working for a different candidate and said so many things disparaging to Trump. Then, when she got to know him, she became one of his fiercest protectors.

This brings up loyalty. Since a young age, Trump has been able to evoke loyalty in those around him. He sees loyalty from a perspective that is very different from the rest of the world. When his father built his company, what was always part of that process was the loyalty that he showed to those who worked for him, and in return, they showed him loyalty as well. Take, for instance, his secretary. She worked for Fred for more than six decades. Can you imagine anyone holding one job or keeping one person employed for this long? It is not common, but that is one of the ways Fred invoked loyalty.

It has been said many times that the kind of loyalty President Trump expects is the kind of loyalty that you find in Puzo's Godfather trilogy. Or the kind of loyalty that mob bosses expect from their foot soldiers. What they don't understand is that loyalty is the tie that binds any strong organization or country. It was the key to Fred's success, and it is something that Trump grew up witnessing firsthand. He knows it works and strictly abides by it.

Trump has grown up to believe that loyalty is a powerful force, and he continues to display it as long as the other side displays it as well. When they stop, he is truly offended. But there are those who think that Trump has no loyalty to others. They cite his many marriages and divorces and the paramours he has been associated with.

Again, the lens through which people see these events is distorted and not the same lens through which he sees it. As for women, he doesn't think his affairs are being disloyal in any way.

The loyalty that a politician needs or a businessman needs for that matter is diametrically opposed to what commoners think of as loyalty. How could a politician in a democracy be loyal to a policy when the public no longer deems it in their best interest? Should the politician enforce his ideals or should he then follow what his constituents want? Think about that while you think about President Trump's behavior. It doesn't matter if he is pro-life at one point in his life or pro-choice. As long as he faithfully executes his constituents' desires, then he is doing his job.

President Trump himself is not opposed to immigration. That much is clear. He has family members who were first-generation immigrants, and two of three wives were immigrants. He himself had a mother and a grandmother who were immigrants. He is a man surrounded by the rich diversity of the American fabric, yet he enforces anti-immigration rules. Why? Because, as a politician, his one loyalty is to his base. That is what he is supposed to do, and that is what he will keep doing.

As he grew up, there was a strong sense of loyalty that was instilled within the family. That was something his father felt was most important. His mother, however, was not steeped in a tradition of loyalty. His mother was more about being self-serving, but there is nothing wrong with that. The whole idea of being effective in this world is to be able to do what serves you the best. Not everyone can be self-sacrificing in the face of a crisis. Even when you are in a plane, the flight attendants will tell you that in the event of rapid decompression and when the masks fall from the top you have to put your mask on first before you put on the mask for your child or infant. That may sound self-serving. In fact, it is, but being self-serving is an important aspect of raising a child.

Trump learned from a young age that loyalty and self-serving tendencies can coexist. He saw his father nurture the loyalty aspect of it, and he saw his mother nurture the self-serving aspect of it. His mind, as powerful as it was, and still is, managed to bring those two seeming inconsistencies together, and what you have at that point is a person who is fungible in his political views—loyal to those who are his base since it is a self-serving kind of loyalty.

As such, what you have is a man who can charm anyone around him and communicate what he wants from them, all while he rewards loyalty and demands it in return. Donald Trump is a rare personality—misunderstood because of his theatrics and showmanship—but effective nonetheless.

As he was constantly asking questions as a child, his mother was not keen on being put on the spot, and she lobbied that he be put in school as soon as possible. They chose the Kew-Forest School in Queens. It is a private school that still operates today and has become one of the better schools to prep for college in New York. Some notable people of American industry attended this school before going on to Ivy League institutions.

Trump was enrolled in a prekindergarten program and was out of the house. In evaluating this experience, Trump was a natural at commanding the acquiescence of his peers even at the age of five—which earned him a reputation for being a bully. He wanted everyone under this thumb—something his father did effortlessly but young Trump didn't know how to do. He mimicked the effect that he saw take place around his father, and he wanted that to happen. When it didn't, he behaved like his mother—threatening and cold. That turned out to be an effective combination. He was a bully, indeed.

What do you get when you have the prowess of a bully and the charm of a prince? You get the creation of gang-like structures—not the kinds of gangs you think would form on the wrong side of the tracks. These gangs were more like packs of school children. Some loved him, and others hated him, which is similar to the political environment that you find today. Trump would never learn to make the haters love him, and he would see there was nothing he could do to make those who loved him hate him. He bullied those who hated him and backed up those who were on his side. Many adults often engage in such grade school dynamics.

Once he did get to school, the smarter students stayed away from him, and he bullied them from afar, but the less smart ones followed him loyally because he would champion their causes. It was a symbiotic relationship. He became their knight in shining armor. He would stand up for them, and he would praise them. In essence, they felt good about being around him. He also wreaked havoc on those who bullied those who were loyal to him. He had their back. In return, they adulated and cherished him, and that's all he wanted.

That formula worked. It was not the formula his father or mother used. It was a formula that Donald Trump himself had come up with by observing the way people behaved around his father and the way his mother behaved around others. It became the brand promise of the Trump name in the years to come.

It was by no means an example of what Fred Trump did or would ever do. Fred Trump cherished a low profile. Mary Anne Trump, however, was the opposite. She would scream her presence from the mountaintop if she could. She had had enough of walking with her head bent down as she scurried through the streets to church with muddy shoes and smelled the stench of fish. She had had enough of rich folk telling her and her family that they couldn't walk on their street. Now she was rich, and she and her chauffeur-driven Rolls-Royce could pass by on any street without fear of being chased away. Trump watched and inculcated that into his routine, which is why he may seem that he has a chip on his shoulder, but he really doesn't. That fake "chip" is the bravado he knows will deter any assault on his position or his interests.

Both his parents were headstrong. Fred, for all his genial and effective ways, was a headstrong businessman and patriarch. Mary Anne was stubborn in her own way, and when you put both brands of the headstrong into one person, what you get is a person like Donald Trump.

Being as headstrong as he is is almost impossible for anyone else. That level of stubbornness only comes from a kind of God complex that psychologists reference. He is so confident of himself and so sure of his invincibility that he feels he can do anything and get away with it.

On top of that, when you add that he always has a group that he is protecting or championing, then the support he gets from that group gives him the legitimacy he feels he needs to break all other rules and codes of conduct.

As a preteen, he experimented with this and found that it worked in his favor. His current behavior is not one that sprouts from arrogance but one that evolved from experience. In the past, before he even left grade school, he found that whenever someone stands up to you, you have to double down, puff your chest out, and push back. His experience tells him that the only thing that the opposition or the enemy can do to you is shame you and threaten you. If you stand up to that and put them down, you will win instead.

By doubling down and not yielding, Trump would get into fights with his classmates. There was a time that he was in a second-floor classroom, and the conversation escalated into a tussle. Both boys were fighting it out and landed up shoving and pushing each other until it came to a point where both were hanging out of the ledge of an open window. If two other seniors hadn't pulled them both out, the fall would have been fatal. He didn't back down even in the face of physical peril because to him losing is worse.

Trump sees errors as weakness and realized when he was young that he always had to be right. He was a bright student and knew what he was talking about. It was a powerful combination. As time passed, he also realized that when strength and knowledge were pit against one another, strength won out. It was more important to him then to be strong rather than right.

That led to the path of evolution that prioritized strength over knowledge, and he was correct in doing so. He gained more followers by being powerful than by being a policy wonk. So whenever he got into a battle, it became more about who was stronger, not who was correct. To make that point, young Trump took on his teachers whenever he needed to just to prove his point to the young followers he had around him. Many of his teachers started to despise his penchant for standing up to them.

He always knew that to end the domination of an opponent you had to weaken what others thought of that person. He shouldn't have written a book on the art of the deal. He should have written the book on the art of dominating your opponent—or the art of war. That ability to dominate went as far back as his youth. There are stories, unconfirmed by this author, that he once slapped his teacher. The point is not whether or not he did it but why he would do it if it indeed did happen. Trump understands that when you decapitate the opponent in the eyes of their supporters you end up either winning over the supporter or seizing the support from your opponent. Human psychology is such that many would support you if you are perceived as the stronger person. Trump succeeded in showing that he was the stronger candidate. That is how he handled his Republican primary. He had a quaint nickname for each of his opponents. None of them could mount an effective comeback, and in time they lost the support of their own supporters.

Whether it was Jeb Bush or Marco Rubio, no one could mount a credible challenge against him, and soon they dropped out one by one. It was never about the policies. As mentioned, Trump doesn't think the smart man always wins. The stronger one does.

It wasn't just limited to a cerebral assessment of the virtues of being strong and brave. Trump was inherently a strong character. He had no fear in him of anything. Part of it came from the confidence he had that his father would get him out of anything, and the other part was because he was just wired that way. In time, fearlessness became a habit.

There was a time when he was playing with his maid in the yard. He was just five years old at that time. They found a tunnel in the back, and it was dark. His curiosity, which always got the better of him, prompted him to enter that tunnel to see where it led. His maid had to fallow him in, and he just kept going regardless of how dark it got. Trump is fearless, which is why he always came out on top. That lack of fear allows him to brave any situation, and since the person who holds on the longest always wins, he lands up always winning.

One characteristic of his childhood that played out on live TV during the debates was when he hovered behind Hillary Clinton. He placed so much stress on her that you could see the discomfort in her face. In fact, a year after the election, she gave an interview in which she referenced the debate where he had hovered around her and mentioned how stressed it made her feel.

Trump is a master at psychologically intimidating his opponent. Those who don't love him for him end up fearing him for this reason. He does that all the time, which is why he thinks that he can do it to such people as Kim Jong-un and other world leaders whom he needs to convince of one thing or another.

In most cases, it works. In his early years at Kew-Forest, he was a solid student. There is a lot of controversy about his grades. It recently came out that he had instructed his personal attorney to send letters to his previous schools and block all requests for his grades.

One could take that to mean that he was a bad student. Most people tend to make that assumption, but that allows him to dominate them. Here is how he gets that to work in his favor.

Consider this possibility. If his grades were so

bad, how was it possible for him to get into the Wharton School at the University of Pennsylvania? He couldn't. So, logic dictates that it is not beyond the possibility that he was an above-average student, and that his grades from Kew-Forest to the time he was at Fordham University must have been good enough to please the admission department. So the question then is this: if his grades are so good or not so bad, depending on how one sees it, then why hide it?

The reason is because it is a power play. When you remove something from purview, it shows that you are not subordinate to that person. It also creates a mystery surrounding that person. Trump essentially hacks into the mind of the opponent by preventing them from seeing and thereby having to guess about their opponent. It's like getting in a room and Trump turns out the lights while he has the advantage because he is wearing night goggles.

By not allowing anyone to see his grades, he tells them that he is above them, and then if they choose to complain about it, they look petty, and if they choose to say that he has bad grades, they can't because they also know that he has been educated at an Ivy League university. He could not have gotten in if he had poor grades. Period.

Either way, he wins. He plays the perfect head game, and people fall for it. The worst that his opponents can do is call him a bully, which he readily accepts.

As for his parents, they couldn't take his

shenanigans any longer. He was out of control. He was the smartest student in school, but he was also the biggest headache to his parents and teachers. His father just wanted him to study the material, and his mother just wanted him to be occupied. Instead, he was causing trouble, partially fueled by his intellect and partially to gain the approval of his father and the attention of his mother.

Chapter 6 The Path

It was finally decided much to the disappointment of his father and the relief of his mother that he needed to be in surroundings with structure and discipline.

They chose to enroll Trump at a military academy. It was partially to introduce discipline to a boy who was headstrong but also partially so that the teacher could wrestle control away from a very strong Trump.

They could have chosen any private school, but they chose a military academy so that they could neutralize the richness of his upbringing and knock some discipline into him. The teachers at NYMA were hands-on in a literal way. They did not hesitate to stand up to face a bully, and this strategy worked.

By the time the Trumps had sent Donald to the Academy, it had become clear that he would only respond to displays of strength. It wasn't the physical abilities of the instructors at NYMA that subdued his tenacity. It was the respect he had for their strength. Trump was and is the quintessential alpha male who understands the dynamics of strength.

In hindsight, it was one of the best things that could have happened to him at the time. When he got there, his shenanigans paused for some time as he got to know his way around the school. He was hazed, but he took it like a man. The strength of body and mind that he showed while under pressure earned him respect, and he began to channel his energy into other areas. It was a highly productive period in his life.

The New York Military Academy was located just a few miles from West Point, but it was not a U.S. government institution. It was a private institution that was mostly attended by young people whose parents could afford to send them to a regimented school but didn't want the rigors of a real military college. The idea was to knock some sense into them and keep them away from home, not to make them into soldiers.

The NYMA experience was something that indeed helped Trump in the end. It was not the kind of help that Mary Anne Trump had envisioned, but it was the kind of surroundings that he needed. Not only was there a structured environment, but it also surrounded him with other teenagers who had a strong mind like his. Just as a comparison to the kind of outcome that the NYMA produced, the same year that Trump attended the NYMA so did such people as Art Davies, founder of the Ultimate Fighting Championship, which is a mixed martial arts promotion company that has gained popularity in the last decade as a competition for the toughest fighters. This was the kind of experience that Trump experienced when he was at NYMA.

The NYMA was not a rowdy and thuggish outfit but filled with boys who had a lot of spirit and were the kinds of people who would go out into the world and make a significant impact. The Art Davies of the world are not the only ones who attended NYMA. John Gotti and composer Charles Sondheim were also there at different times. These were all alpha males, and such surroundings had a positive influence on the teenage Trump.

The year after he was elected to the presidency Trump wrote to the headmaster of the Academy and commended him on how strong they used to be and that they should not back off from that version of themselves. In other words, he saw the benefit they offered in the strength they displayed. Trump responds positively to strength. He despises weakness and will crush a person whom he thinks is weak, as many of his cabinet secretaries can attest to.

President Trump arrived at NYMA in 1959 when he was thirteen years old. He stayed there until he was eighteen. His classmates remember that he had an average build when he arrived, but he soon developed more physically.

He played football, baseball, and soccer and was good at all three. Many trophies and awards from this period of his life bear his name. The reason he did well in all these sports is not as many would think attributable to any natural athletic ability but because he was naturally competitive.

Trump felt compelled to win at everything he

was involved in. It was never enough for him to come in second place. That wasn't just something he learned. It seemed that his desire to always be on top was always what drove him, and he had the energy to keep up and be on top.

He was so competitive that most people believed he would end up playing sports professionally, even his coaches. By the time he was fifteen, he had morphed into a handsome, charming, and eloquent young man. He was tall and muscular. He was also a stickler for detail, which showed in his appearance. His hair was always neatly "coiffed," as FBI Director Comey would come to notice the first time they met. He was always meticulous about his appearance, and he was given a medal for the best-dressed cadet. Coming from a military academy where everyone is required to be meticulously dressed that says a lot.

Of course, Trump is not perfect. None of us are, but where we fail because we have a sense of arbitrary rules to follow that may diminish our ability to win or succeed, he excels. He has no guardrails that tell him he can't do something. For him, he has to win at all costs, which has been part of his personality and character since he was five.

The moment he got to NYMA that characteristic expanded and took on more seriousness and covered a larger segment of his life, his thinking, and his outlook. He found a home amidst the others who attended the Academy. He had been forced by his parents to leave the luxury of the family home at the age of thirteen, and that vexed him deeply. He was glad to be with friends and among boys his own age and personality (back then it was not a coed institution that it is today).

The irritation he harbored with being sent away and not allowed to return during the school year even though he was just an hour's drive away didn't sit well with him. What made it worse was that he knew his mother wanted more than anyone else for him to be out of the house. He came to find out that it was his mother who instigated his expulsion from home, and that his father agreed only because he believed it would be good for him. What he despised was that his mother just wanted to have an easier life and enjoy her wealthy lifestyle. During the first two years of his presidency, the credenza behind the Resolute Desk only held a photograph of his father. His mother's image wouldn't appear until almost two years later.

His childhood visions of loving his mother slowly began to fade, and by the time he graduated from the Academy in 1964, he had placed her in the rear-view mirror. Mother and son both lost out. The mother lost a son who truly loved her and looked up to her, and the son lost the value of a mother's teaching in a young man's life. A mother brings empathy and the value of love to a young boy so that when he grows up he is able to show compassion and empathy to those around him.

Contrary to the belief that Trump's detractors

espouse, Trump is not a disorganized person. He is actually a highly secretive person. What seems to be disorganized and lazy is actually his way of getting things done. Each person in an organization brings different skill sets to the table. Trump doesn't believe that those skill sets need to be replicated or duplicated. He looks at it as he would in such sports as football or baseball. There is only one of each position and only one head coach. The one with the most strategic mind and the most intuition is the one who becomes the head coach. He sees himself as that person.

In everything he does, there aren't different layers to an organization. He doesn't need thousands of workers to make his business work. He just needs everyone doing what they do best, and he will add value to the table by giving them his insight, intuition, and intelligence.

As president, much has been said about him and his "Executive Time." Most people tend to think of his time that is unstructured as time that is wasted and not doing the job that the people elected him to do. Most people have that wrong. The more intelligent the person and the more intuitive their skills, the less structured they need to be to be able to do better at what they do. When he was at the Academy and this goes all the way back to when he was just starting off as a teenager, he got more done in less time than his fellow classmates, but he never got it done during the scheduled times. Part of Trump's genius is his ability to solve issues that others can't because of the way he thinks. His solutions are beyond cerebral. They are intuitive and most often right.

During his time at the Academy, he rose to the rank of Captain of Supplies, which, in context, was the third-highest ranking officer in the entire Academy. He got there the same way he achieved everything else after he left—with courage and intuition.

Then there is the power he has over other people's reality. Trump has always had the ability to alter the reality around him and those beside him. It started sometime at the Academy and has persisted all through his career. The only other person that most people know who could do that was the late Steve Jobs. These men had the unique gift of being able to alter the perception and the reality of the present moment. They could make you and all those around you believe that the sun was out and the sky was blue while you were getting drenched in the pouring rain.

This phenomenon came to be known as a Reality Distortion Field, an homage to force fields and the line in sci-fi stories, such as *Star Trek*. People with this ability would be able to distort reality and the perception of that reality just by the sheer force of their personality.

The ages between thirteen and eighteen are very important to a boy. It forms the personality and the template of his adult life and is often irreplaceable and unchangeable. The trajectory that a man takes over the course of his life is very much dependent on the initial arc that he scribes, which is one reason why coed institutions are good for adolescents, especially when they are in a boarding school environment. The mixed crowd brings the knowledge of diversity in strength and the spectrum of human characteristics across genders.

As he no longer saw his mother as a force in his life and that she didn't convey empathy during the time he looked up to her points to the possibility that he had no way of processing the role of women and the contributions they make to society as a whole. In typical homes and during normal childhood strategies, it is the mother who provides the love and empathy that children learn to adopt.

If that relationship is soured or severed, then the ability to learn from one's mother—the softer side of the equation—becomes unavailable, and the countervailing forces that determine the child's development are left to one's primal and base instincts. Those who harness their base instincts and primal powers typically play by the rules of the jungle where the alpha male leads, and everyone else follows. That was the natural order of things for Trump from the very beginning.

Trump is not the metrosexual many men are these days because he never learned the balance that most men adapt to when they are brought up by a woman in the family and socialize with women as equals at school. Instead, he tipped over to the primal side of the equation and formed a lens from which he saw women as something lesser in strength.

That does not mean he thinks women are incapable. He has learned along the way that women can be smart and accomplished, but he also believes at the back of his mind that women need the guidance of a man. He treats his daughters the same way. He gives his son-in-law more forum than his daughter. He thinks that a woman's role is to be attractive and at the pleasure of the man. To him, that is not disparaging in any way. It is just the natural order of things. It is also the reason why he doesn't see anything wrong when he walks into the changing room of pageant contestants unannounced. He acknowledges that women can be smart and productive, but their first responsibility is to look attractive.

One can't blame him for this attitude. It is just the way he sees things. It was part of the collective thinking of society back then, and it is what he observed at home.

Chapter 7 The Power

Gene Roddenberry, the creator of *Star Trek*, wrote one of the original stories for the first season that aired in 1966. In one of the last episodes of the season, which was a great hit back then, an alien species created a world just by using the powers of their mind. In essence, they took the concept of mind over matter to the next level and created matter out of the powers of the mind. It was called the reality distortion field and meant that reality was being distorted by a field—similar to a magnetic or electrical field, but in this case, it was a mental field. This field would then distort reality as the rest of us perceived it.

Since then the term has only been applied once with any real success. It is to be found in Walter Isaacson's biography of Steve Jobs, the late cofounder of Apple. Not many men can do this, although many motivation and life coach gurus have tried to teach others to do it, although they themselves have no idea how to convincingly pull it off.

Most people can easily describe it and determine what it takes to do it, but only a few people know how to actually do it in a way that works. The first person that we know of is the aforementioned Steve Jobs. The second person that we know of—someone who took that skill to a level so expansive that it feels surreal in most situations—is Donald Trump, President of the United States.

In a world that is driven by finite points of data, it is hard to fathom the power and effect of something like the reality distortion field. Yet, evidence suggests that it works. By the time President Trump had graduated, he was well aware of the power of distortion and the effect it had on him personally and on all those around him. It was almost like a spell that he could cast over a wide area.

There was a particular incident during his senior year. Graduation was around the corner, and it was one of the last times many friends would be able to see each other regularly. During a conversation while they were walking, Trump and a friend were passing the baseball pitch, when Trump asked the other person to tell him about a time he (Trump) was super on the pitch.

The other boy thought it was an odd request because someone doesn't often ask you to relate a story about themselves. But that was his way. The other boy started telling him how the bases were loaded, and that Trump was the batter who hit the ball over the pitcher's head and the team won. Trump smiled, stopped the other boy, turned to him, and said, "I hit it out of the park. Remember that. It was a home run, and I hit it out of the park." He hadn't. The boy was right. It had actually gone right over the pitcher's head.

The boy froze for a moment as Trump stopped

smiling, turned an ugly shade of seriousness, and glared straight into his eyes. The boy instantly recanted his story and said that Trump was right. It was indeed hit out of the park, and he thereafter forgot what really happened. From then on whenever he told the story, he always remembered it, or at least told the story that Trump had hit the ball out of the park. That story persisted for more than fifty years.

One must take two things from that incident to be able to help decipher the way Trump works and the way those around him behave: (1) Trump has the power to make people alter their memory. When Sean Spicer comes to the podium on the first day of his job and tells White House reporters that the crowd that attended the inauguration was the biggest crowd that had ever gathered for an inauguration, he meant it. Spicer honestly believed it, and in his mind at the time, he didn't come close to thinking that the reality was not the same as his perception. He had been through the reality distortion field. He is not the only one. When you hear Trump's counselor, Kellyanne Conway, talk about alternative facts, what she is saying is that she sees things the way Trump has projected them to be, and they believe it wholeheartedly.

(2) Trump has the need to make his already good achievements seem better than they were. It was good enough to win the baseball game. The ball didn't need to be out of the park, but Trump needed others to remember it that way. For most people, winning the competition would have been enough. It didn't need to be the

largest crowd ever. Winning the presidency would have been good enough for most but not for Trump. For him, not only did he want to win it, but he also wanted to win it big—if not in reality, at least in his mind.

There are a few elements that a person needs to be able to successfully pull off the reality distortion field. Whether that is used to win a presidential election or get a bank loan, the power of reality distortion is something that we all inherently try to do but fail miserably.

What is the reality distortion field in actuality? As commentators have put it and so have pop psychologists, the reality distortion field is the effect that a person has on people and events that happen around him. To be able to pull it off, the person doing it has to have a unique combination of skills and certainly able to be charming.

To be charming, one has to have two qualities. The first is believing that people truly like them. If a person has any notion whatsoever that the world in general does not like them, then the ability to be charming is diminished. They will just be cynical inside.

In some cases, if that belief is chiseled away until it no longer exists, then the ability to be charming will also erode to the point of depression and seclusion. In the case of Donald Trump, he has significant charm because he believes that others have significant appreciation for his intelligence, his good looks, and his charisma.

Charisma and charm almost sound like the same thing, but they aren't. Charisma is the confidence one exhibits in one's ability to do anything. A person with strong charisma is confident to the nth degree. That charisma then feeds into the ability to be charming, and the circle keeps going around.

In time, the person learns that the ability to maintain his charisma affects his charm, and the ability to be charming also depends on his charisma. They are mutually dependent. They also learn that if they are out of one the other soon dissipates as well. So, how to ignite them back to being charismatic? You can do one of two things. You can either surround yourself with people who will cheer you on and listen to anything you have to say, or you say things that may not be true but are good enough to lift your spirits until you recover your charisma and charm.

But that alone is insufficient to be a person who can warp reality across an entire spectrum of people. People with this ability, such as Jobs and Trump, are those who have significant levels of courage.

We can look at this courage in two ways: (1) a person fears an event or an object but learns to suppress that fear and learns strategies to overcome its effects on themselves.

(2) the kind of person who has no discernible concept of fear in their psyche. Their ability to stay above and relevant is in the conscious part of their brain and not in the primal area. They

see the lack of bravado or bravery as a larger threat to their existence than the safety that healthy levels of fear may give them. Most people relegate the fear center of the brain to the central portion of their thinking, meaning that it is always online in all things we do. People like Trump have managed to rewire their fear center and remove it from their conscious path.

We need people like this—people who have no sense of fear in anything they do. Much of the world as we know it has been built by men who have not known what fear feels like or needed the adrenaline that fear can induce. Fear is a powerful motivator and an oppressor. How one controls it depends on how they are wired.

Some people are wired in such a way that they have this heightened sense of preservation, so they fear everything. It is counterintuitive and counterproductive because in the end it is that fear that prevents them from doing so much more. It is also a self-fulfilling prophecy. Whatever one fears usually comes to fruition.

Then there is the second consequence of fear, which is when people get so tired of the stress that fear places on them that they find ways to be strong. They redefine their fear and stand up to it. These are the two camps that most people fall into.

But then there is a third situation where the person feels no fear and is just strong and brave in all circumstances. This kind of strength is actually dangerous, and most people do not have this kind of strength. If they did, the species might not last long. At the same time, it is this kind of strength when applied to the right set of circumstances that results in people who change the course of the world—good or bad—but they literally take the world by its horns and wrestle it to its feet. Then they remake that world in their own image. There have been only a few such people like this in history. Genghis Khan is one of them, and Trump is another.

Many of the characteristics that Genghis Khan displayed in the course of his conquests show a level of fearlessness—evidence of a person's lack of fear. It should be noted that this lack of fear in people can sometimes lead to suboptimal outcomes. Fear has a benefit that most people just need. It allows us to trigger the fight or flight response within us, and that allows us to seek the higher ground in safety or to wage a battle that vanquishes the threat. But when one gets into a situation where they can't invoke fear or feel fear, then the ability to trigger the superhuman force of fight or flight is suppressed. This is the reason it is dangerous for most people to be fearless except for such people as Trump.

Have you ever been able to run faster or do something that required greater strength that you didn't think you had but were able to do it when you were angry or upset? That's the adrenaline of a fight or flight response kicking in. It also has the ability to fine-tune the brain and get the mind to perform at a higher level, but if you are the kind of person who has no fear, then you will miss the benefits of the boost you get when fear kicks in.

That applies for 98 percent of the people. The other 2 percent—people such as Genghis Khan and Donald Trump—can pull the adrenaline and fine-tune their fighting senses at will and do not need the element of fear to invoke that almost superhuman power.

When it is unabated by fear, this kind of strength is one of the elements of reality distortion. People who can rouse armies and nations are said to have this ability to distort reality for their troops and eventually for themselves.

Until this point, we have looked at three of the characteristics that are needed to be able to make the reality distortion field manifest in one's surroundings. We have also seen and evidenced through these actions that President Trump has all three qualities in abundant quantity.

Finally, there is the last element that is required to be successful. It is the element of hyperbole. Trump has always known the value of hyperbole. He realized a long time ago during his days at Kew-Forest that the power of hyperbole can cross the chasm of intelligence.

When someone is a little slow to understand or knows less compared to you, you have to use a little exaggeration and hyperbole to communicate a sense of urgency or motivation. Otherwise, the intended message just falls flat. It's like talking to a child.

President Trump is an expert at hyperbole and has realized that for him to be perceived as the man on top of things many of his already great accomplishments need to be exaggerated. It is better than trying to explain the merits of a win. Telling someone ten years down the road that Trump won the baseball game will fall flat, but telling them that he hit the ball out of the park will resonate and attract applause.

Not only does it cross the chasm of intelligence, but it also crosses the depths of time. It makes him a hero in the eyes of lesser mortals at the time it happened and decades later.

The power of the reality distortion field is well documented. Steve Jobs was able to build a company like Apple (twice) by this mere ability. He could take a company that started out as a project in the garage and financed by the sale of an old VW Bus to be the world's most valuable company within one generation. Donald Trump did the same thing in one generation as well. He took the name of an immigrant family and put it on the roof of the world and on many of glamorous building projects and made himself a billionaire in the eyes of the whole world.

Chapter 8 The Paradigm

President Trump has attributed his meteoric rise to two factors external to his own inherent abilities. The first was the New York Military Academy. He credits their tough discipline as the way to mold any man.

It is said that such men as Trump do not respect weakness. That is not entirely accurate. He doesn't respect weakness when it applies to those he associates with. It doesn't bother him at all if a person outside his sphere is weak. He categorizes that weak person as a benefit because it becomes easier to command and dictate. As for people within his own sphere, however, then it is totally different. Again, look at the cabinet secretaries and chiefs of staff that have come and gone.

The prerequisite to being able to spread a blanket of alternate reality over a wide swath of people is strength, hyperbole, charisma, and charm. President Trump has all these things. He has had them since he was in NYMA, and it is there that he perfected them and advanced them.

That Realty Distortion Field, aside from placing him at the top of the world, has another specific advantage. It enhances the perception of his brand. His wealth and property are directly tied to his brand. The more his brand is perceived to be good, the more value is ascribed to it. The more it is valued, the more he is worth. The valuations on his brand are stratospheric. There are numerous buildings that he does not own, but they hoist his name to the top of the building and because it is a Trump Tower, people are willing to pay the developers more for it. The more people are willing to pay for a piece of that tower, the more the developers are willing to pay him to license his name for the building.

This Reality Distortion Field is a major aspect of his ability to garner and hold on to the support of a large number of Americans, but it doesn't stop there. He can distort his accomplishments and leverage them just as he did with his baseball accomplishments. When he does that, it increases his brand, but is that honest? Are his detractors right in saying that he is untruthful?

In most cases, the media has labeled him as untruthful. That's both sides of the media. The liberal and the conservative media have both called him a liar and a cheat. He is neither of those things if you look at it in the proper context.

Let's take his 2016 opponent for instance. Hillary Clinton is the exact opposite of Donald Trump in this regard. She is a person who would tell the truth but seem to be lying, while he would tell a lie and have the crowd believe. There is great power in that.

When he was in the Academy, he learned that there are different ranks in the military and different strata of society. The highest rank that has the least number of people know most of the information. The lowest rank that covers the most people know the least. That is the best way to manage information. It keeps everything intact. It's similar to telling your child that everything is okay even though an intruder is trying to break in. You keep the truth because you don't want to get them in a state where they may become irrational and overwhelmed with fear.

For someone who has no fear but just understands that others do have the potential to be clouded by fear, it occurs to them that the truth is not always a good thing. Which would bring the greater good—telling a toddler that his mother has a terminal ailment or to say that mommy is fine?

The next problem is inconsistency. When you try to tell the truth sometimes and lie at other times, what happens? It tends to backfire. What he learned repeatedly in his teenage years was that you can't lie once in a while. To be convincing all the time, you have to lie all the time. Even for things that don't matter.

Armchair psychiatrists will jump to call it pathological. Maybe. But look at the facts a little more. The pattern of a pathological liar is someone who is good at lying. They are professionals. You can think of a spy as a pathological liar because they are so good at lying that even they don't know they are lying, or rather they can't be caught even by a lie detector.

As you can tell, Trump is not that way. He embellishes so much that you can pick out some of his lies. When he obviously goes out of his way to lie, it confuses the person listening to him until they overload on what they know and don't know about him.

On the other hand, Donald Trump is one of the most honest politicians you will find in Washington, D.C. because he tells it like it is. He has always said what he needs to to get on top of the situation.

This has held true since he was at the military academy, and it holds true even now. In the midst of President Obama's first term, it had occurred to Trump that a bureaucrat in office would not be able to pass muster. He had thought seriously about running against Obama in the 2012 election.

It turns out that he didn't have any personal views of Obama, but he just thought that he could do a better job. He then contacted David Bossie, who was head of the infamous Citizens United and an ardent critic of the Clintons. Bossie was willing to meet with Trump and asked a friend—a fellow Citizens United patriot—Steve Bannon—to tag along.

Initially, Steve was not interested, but Bossie made it compelling, and Steve agreed to go, although he was not interested for two reasons: (1) running against Obama was suicide, and (2) Trump had made overtures to run in the past but never followed through. Bannon thought it would be a waste of time, which was time he didn't have. He decided to go, however, and the two of them went to New York City and headed up to the conference room on the 26th floor of Trump Tower.

The first presentation that Bossie made was to get Trump to run against Obama in the upcoming general election. Bannon thought it was a bad idea. In fact, he thought the whole thing was just a waste of time and a joke. He hadn't known Trump for long and thought this wouldn't go anywhere. Bannon was hard core. He was all about the cause and an ardent Tea Party kind of person. He thought Trump was the exact opposite of what was needed to put up a challenge to Obama and, more importantly, to Clinton, who was certainly going to be the candidate in 2016.

They tried to dissuade Trump by talking about the conservative movement and how the conservative platform was totally and diametrically opposed to the liberal platform. If the conservative movement was to the right, the Tea Party movement was right of that.

They said Trump's original and repeatedly stated policies were in direct opposition to that. Bossie was trying to get a candidate to ride the Tea Party wave. Trump's response was that he could do that. He asked about their platform. When they told him that they were strictly pro-life, he instantly jumped on and said he was pro-life too. Then Bannon interjected and said that he had been a pro-choice advocate all his life, and he had repeatedly donated to pro-life candidates.

Trump responded, "That can be fixed. You just tell me how to fix that. I am . . . what do you call it? Pro-life? Well, I'm that. I'm pro-life, I'm telling you."

Trump always knew how to be whatever he needed to be. It was all part of that reality distortion skill he possessed. It took some time after that, but Bossie and Bannon were impressed. Even though they decided that 2012 would not be the year for it to happen, they would definitely make the 2016 run.

The point is that candidate Trump repeatedly said he supported policies that were essentially Democratic and liberal. The moment the time came to run in the election, he switched his policy and stuck with the policy that he needed to embrace to be able to represent his base.

Was that a lie? No. He became who he needed to be to represent a group of people that he thought would best be served by him. It is not different from when Hillary moved to New York so that she could run as the senator from New York. She was originally from Chicago and then Arkansas, but she moved to New York to take on New York issues and New York values. In the same way, Trump moved from the liberal part of the spectrum to the conservative part of it.

This is not the track of a pathological liar. This is a man wanting to be a populist. He says what he needs to say to get what he wants. Once the audience understands that, they will come to decipher the code that he speaks. If you listen to every speech or every conversation he has, he is straight up about everything except when he wants to throw the opponent off his scent. The harder he pushes just means the harder he is trying to push the other person off their track.

There is no such thing as an honest politician. Trump's honesty is not the issue. It's his ability to win. He has always been a winner. From the time he was in grade school to the time he was at the Academy and beyond, he was always focused on coming out ahead. His time at NYMA hardened his ability to get what he wanted by saying what he needed to. There was no policy so stringent that he could not alter it so that he could eventually win.

By the time Trump made it to college, he had a new way about him. He was no longer the man he had started out to be. He started out by emulating his father. By this point in his life, he was nothing like Fred. Fred was hardworking, while Donald was skating on his charm and super intelligence.

He had no intention to go to college. He was not interested in partying or studying. It was all a waste of time. His grandfather and his father were successful men in their own right, and neither of them ever needed a degree or any form of higher education. He believed the Trump men were above that, and he was right.

Colleges only pollute the brain with group-think. Such men as the Trumps, from Fred Sr., to Fred

Jr. and now to Donald, were never part of that. They were intelligent and hardworking men who were intelligent by their own means and used their uniquely wired brain to achieve the end result.

It was by his own admission that Trump went to college and one that was branded. The Wharton School, which has consistently held one of the top three positions in the rankings for business schools over the last decade and beyond, was just about as good as the branding could get. As far as Trump was concerned, that didn't matter. He was there for a certificate. It was about attaching his name and brand to the brand of the Wharton School.

The Wharton School today attracts the highest minds coming out of high school from around the country and the rest of the world. They have a solid program in economics, business, and commerce, and it is considered a competitive college to get into. It holds the record for the highest GMAT scores for entry and the top- ten highest scores for standardized tests for those entering a four-year program.

Trump's opponents constantly insinuate that he made it in because of his father's donation. That is both an insult to his intelligence and, more importantly, it is contemptible to suggest that the highest-ranking school in the country would stoop to such a level. Even if that were true, the point is that Trump contends that he learned more from experience than he did from sitting in a lecture hall.

When Trump was at Wharton, he spent most weekends traveling. Sometimes he made it back for class on Monday, and sometimes he didn't. To put this in context, the acceptance rate for the Wharton school at around the time that Trump transferred in was about 25 percent for freshmen and much lower for transfers. He had come in from Fordham University—again because of the branding.

He had already started taking on deals by the time he was at Wharton. That was what interested him more than anything else. He wanted to do the deals, and he wanted to make money. Studies and drafts were a distraction and a waste of time.

He hardly spent any time in college. He was usually out trying to close a deal or do something more productive (his words). Nothing about sitting in a classroom and learning theory appealed to him. Trump has always been a man of action. He has always wanted to get knee-deep in it and get his hands dirty.

Why, then, did he go to college? The answer is two-fold. The first was about the brand of the university, but a serious student of history and reasoning would then ask that if it was always about branding why did he go to Fordham first?

Therein comes the second reason behind his decision to go to college—to make his father happy. By this point, Fred was very successful in the tri-state area. Money was not the problem, and he wanted his son to have an education or something that he didn't have due to his father's untimely passing.

So he transferred that desire on to his son. Money was not an object in his desire to see his son graduate in cap and gown, and Fordham was just as good a school as any. When the time came, however, Donald realized that if he had to endure the rigors of school it might as well be worth it. The time it took would be the same, but the benefit of a branded certificate would raise his own brand.

One other aspect of Trump's psyche is that it's all about branding. Trump's father was more than happy to pay the extra that it cost to put him through a good school, and with his blessing and a new Ford convertible, young Donald drove down to Philadelphia and got himself situated in one of the top schools in the country. He was there in his suit and with a briefcase, which the students back then remember—albeit mockingly.

He may have been a little overdressed, but he was there dressed to the hilt, and he meant business. Just as in the days at the Academy, Trump was here to work and to look the part.

During his time at the Academy, he won awards for his dress and neatness, and that didn't change when he got to Wharton. Some people thought he was geeky, but he didn't care. He was there for a very different reason than they were. They were there to learn the ABCs of business and economics, but he already knew all of that. He was far ahead of the game.

Just like Bill Gates who left Harvard ahead of

time because he had more to accomplish than what Harvard could offer and how Mike Zuckerberg left Harvard before graduation, none of these superstars needed to learn what they already knew from real life. At least in Trump's case, he stayed to please his dad.

On the day of his graduation, he stood wearing the cap and gown, trimmed with the gold band that signified the school he was graduating from. Everyone was wearing the traditional black cap and gown but had different bands depending on the school they came from. The School of Arts and Science had one color. The Wharton School had yellow.

He had made it across the finish line. He got what he wanted—the scroll emblazoned with the brand that would help launch his career. Along the way, he had learned a few things here and there. He felt it was nice to have those but not necessary and certainly not worth the time he had spent getting it. If he had been able to be out in the world and making his mark, he would have learned more in terms of experience and made more in terms of money.

Trump always felt that he learned the most—the experiences that made him who he is—at the NY Military Academy. That was all he needed. By comparison, Wharton was just not that important.

Schools exist to prepare most people for jobs. As much as they say they do, schools do not create leaders. Leaders—true leaders—are born and bludgeoned by their own desires to become true leaders. They are surrounded by inspiring men and learn from them. Trump learned from Fred, who was his guiding light. Fred was his road map. He didn't just want to be like Fred. He wanted to be better. Trump always believed, and rightfully so, that his job was to emulate his father and then take it further. But that leap from his father's shoulders was not meant to be in competition with his father but rather as an homage to him.

As he stood to pose for the countless photographs to memorialize his graduation, he towered over his parents, looking exceptionally groomed and smart but punctuated the scene with a sullen look—a look of discomfort at not knowing what would come next. It was 1968. The war in Vietnam was raging. The day he graduated America faced one if its most gruesome days on the battlefield. More than sixteen thousand soldiers had died. The draft was in full swing, and his turn was coming.

Chapter 9 The Battlefront

Four decades later our perception of the Vietnam War is a product of the mosaic of information that we have accumulated over time. We are caught between truth and loyalty, which are both powerful elements of one's soul. We take for granted that truth and loyalty are always on the same side and are at peace with that. Then, ever so often, events come along that truth and loyalty come to rest on opposing sides.

The Vietnam War was such an event.

What may have started out in the interest of the country proceeded against the will of the people. The '70s saw countless protests and movements opposing the premise of the war and the battles themselves, but four decades later and in the time that has passed in between, we find ourselves in a bind. We are unable to criticize the war or the reasons that we got into it because we do not want to diminish the valor that was displayed by the men and women who lost their lives and the families who lost their loved ones.

The truth is, though, that the war was unnecessary, but our loyalty to it and its people who sacrificed everything keeps us from saying anything. But there is a way of going about that. For all the men and women who gave their last full measure of devotion, our appreciation for their action symbolizes our loyalty, but we don't have to agree with the politics or the decision-making process that led to the war.

The Vietnam War was a conflict that included the United States and divided Vietnam—North and South Vietnam. It began on November 1, 1955, and ended approximately nineteen and a half years later on April 30, 1975. Smaller combatants included South Korea, New Zealand, and Australia, all of whom suffered negligible casualties compared with the main participants.

At the end of the war, two million civilians had died, some being from North Vietnam and others from South Vietnam. It resulted in the defeat of South Vietnam, and then a unified communist Vietnam resulted. The communist north had succeeded in their campaign to turn the two halves communist.

One out of every ten Americans of that generation were sent over there. Fifty-four thousand Americans died. Over three hundred thousand were severely injured or crippled. These were horrible odds, and for a man who sees the bottom line, the rationale for these kinds of losses was unpalatable.

Other countries that participated included the Soviet Union and the People's Republic of China, or PRC, led by communist leader Mao Tse-tung. These countries aided North Vietnam in their fight against capitalist South Vietnam but were not warring participants. They merely supplied resources to the PAVN, or the People's Army of Vietnam, the army of North Vietnam.

Two of the largest controversies of the late '60s and early '70s included the war in Vietnam and the draft to man that war. The battles that took place in this tropical country placed a large toll on lives, but sometimes considered worse was the debilitating and shocking injuries that resulted from the kind of warfare that was taking place.

While the death toll was high in absolute numbers, they were on par percentage-wise to other wars the United States had been involved in. The injury rate, however, was three times as high. The physical crippling of young men who went there and the subsequent mental trauma that resulted from the war was higher than any other war in which the U.S. had participated.

President Trump has always felt that the war was ill conceived and poorly executed. He has been against many of the wars that the U.S. has been a part of, as he has not seen the wisdom of American citizens dying on foreign soil to solve a problem that could be diplomatically resolved or won with tactical munitions.

It has been his principle not to fight in these wars, and it has been his resolve to stay away for some time. He dodged the draft five times, doing so each time for a valid reason. It was no different from what Rockefeller did by paying someone to take his place while he felt it was in the best interest of everyone concerned that he stay out of the war. JP Morgan did the same. He, too, paid $300 for someone to take his place during the Civil War. Andrew Carnegie also paid someone to fight in his stead—somewhere in the region of $850. It was not uncommon for those kinds of men to find that their worth to the country was better served doing what they did instead of picking up a rifle. It is especially that way when you think about the Vietnam War as something that many people back then opposed.

Before the Vietnam War, the communist PAVN was the army that defended Vietnam from Japanese occupation. The Japanese had already driven out the French who had ruled Vietnam since the late 1800s, but the people didn't want the Japanese either.

Frankly, they wanted neither the French nor the Japanese to rule them. They wanted to be an independent country. After the Japanese were defeated in the First World War, the French returned to Vietnam in 1945, intending to regain control of Vietnam.

Still united and with the PAVN as their army, the country fought against the French. For the next nine years until 1954, battles were fought between the PAVN and French forces. The Vietnamese controlled a large percentage of North Vietnam, while the French controlled the southern region.

The United States supported and assisted the

French. Their aid, however, was not military aid but rather financial. Under the Eisenhower administration, the United States provided the French with $500 million a year to support their fight against the North Vietnamese. Despite this help, the French were defeated by Vietnamese forces in 1954, marking the end of the First Indochina War. It also established Vietnam's independence. None of this had anything to do with America or Americans, as Trump has repeatedly said.

The Geneva Conference of 1954 temporarily settled the matter by dividing the country into North and South Vietnam. They divided the land along the 17th parallel. The border was set but was supposed to be removed after elections could be held in 1956 to decide what would happen to Vietnam. Would Vietnam become fully communist or fully capitalist? That was the question they were willing to leave to the people in a referendum.

One of the principal causes for the division of Vietnam into north and south was because the northerners wished to be a Communist people and for their entire country to unite under the communist ways of China and the Soviet Union. The inhabitants of the south, however, wished to embrace capitalism. They were also strongly anti-communist. It was pretty much the same division of north and south in Vietnam then as it is now in North and South Korea.

Despite the 1954 Geneva accords, the 1956

elections were never held. In 1955, Ngo Dinh Diem, with massive support from the United States, rose to power and became president of South Vietnam in 1955. After his rise to power, he canceled the 1956 elections and consolidated his position.

Diem's rise to power was greatly supported by the United States under the Eisenhower administration. Although Diem was a corrupt and tyrannical leader, the United States supported him because of his strong opposition to communism. This was something else that Trump never warmed up to. He was never interested in the rationale behind the war. Vietnam was half a world away, with no benefit to the country at home or its people.

Over there, Diem was prepared to exile, imprison, or execute anyone who cooperated with communist bodies or was a communist themselves. Diem was not very popular among the Vietnamese people. His tyrannical and dictatorial rule would eventually lead to his assassination in November 1963. His assassination was carried out through a CIA-funded and supported coup led by General Duong Van Minh. Diem and his regime would then be succeeded by General Duong Van Minh as leader of Vietnam during the rest of the war. Although they overthrew the U.S.-backed dictatorial Ngo Dinh Diem, they were equally as corrupt. Regardless, they received massive support from the United States due to their strong opposition to communism.

This is also something that the idealistic young Trump could not tolerate. He was not sure that all that duplicity was worth the trouble. He said so repeatedly and has since that time derided the policy of nation building, a term that is a euphemism for interfering.

The Americans had interfered with the elections by supporting Diem and making efforts to prevent the 1956 elections from taking place. They did so because they feared that if elections were held the communists might win. Regardless of their reasons, however, it was hypocritical of them. When Joseph Stalin, the former leader of the USSR, prohibited free elections from taking place in countries occupied by the Soviet Union in eastern Europe, Americans were very opposed and repulsed by Stalin's actions, but then they did exactly that.

Diem was a strict and imposing Catholic and looked down on all other religions. One of his activities that unveiled his cruel evangelistic ways was his torment and destruction of the Buddhists in South Vietnam. This led to the self-immolation of the Buddhist monk Thich Quang Duc in protest of Diem's actions against the Buddhists.

This inspired American Norris Morrison to follow Thich Quang Duc's protest by burning himself alive at the Pentagon just below Secretary of Defense Robert McNamara's office.

Morrison's self-immolation was in protest of the United States' involvement in the war.

One of the principal causes for U.S. involvement in the war was their fear and opposition to communism. Americans had always done their best to keep themselves and the Western Hemisphere safe from communism. They felt that if Vietnam fell to communism then the other countries in the area would also fall. They referred to this as the "domino theory," which was coined by U.S. President Eisenhower. It was meant to explain the domino-like effect that would take place if Vietnam fell to communism. The list of dominoes predicted that if Vietnam fell to communism, then Laos, Cambodia, Thailand, Malaysia, Indonesia, Burma, and even India would also fall one after the other. American involvement in the Vietnam War was not just to protect Vietnam alone from communism but was also part of America's main goal to prevent the spread of communism. That theory didn't pan out. Even though Vietnam succumbed to communism, the other Southeast Asian countries remained democratic, once again proving that Trump's outlook was right even when he was just twenty-two years old.

When Dwight David Eisenhower was President of the United States, he already tried to blow out the fire that was the impending war between communist North and capitalist South Vietnam. John Fitzgerald Kennedy, who was a senator at the time, argued that the United States should avoid intervention at all costs. Trump was aligned with Kennedy's thinking at the time.

When Kennedy became president, he would merely support the South Vietnamese with financial aid but would not authorize the firing of a single American bullet at a Viet Minh fighter.

As mentioned earlier, the ARVN was supported by the United States, although involvement from the USA stretched as far back as the Truman administration. Under Truman, small numbers of troops were sent to Vietnam to support the French in their fight against the communist army of Vietnam. Then, under Kennedy, more troops and military personnel were sent to train South Vietnamese ARVN soldiers.

Operation Ranch Hand was the deployment of the chemical weapon known as Agent Orange on the North Vietnamese. United States Air Force planes would fly over North Vietnam and spray the chemical. The effects were devastating. Agent Orange was, aside from a painful way to go, a defoliant or herbicide. Much of the forests were destroyed, and the wildlife population dropped severely. In addition, many people, including civilians, were killed, and many more were seriously wounded. It was so potent that it would burn like acid down to the bone once it came in contact with someone's skin.

Those who were lucky to survive suffered many injuries. The chemical was able to alter the genes of those affected. Generations that came from the survivors of Operation Ranch Hand and the Vietnam War suffered massive deformities, both physical and mental limitations as well as poor health. Today, hundreds of children in Vietnam still suffer from the consequences of Agent Orange.

The methods used during the war in Vietnam were unconscionable to Trump, and he was opposed to everything that had to do with the war. He was opposed to the reason behind it, the methods that were used to fight in it, and the cost to continue waging it, both in terms of human lives and dollars spent. None of it made sense to the young and intelligent Trump.

During Operation Ranch Hand, the deployment of Agent Orange spilled over into Laos. This was caused by American planes spraying Agent Orange along the border between North Vietnam and Laos because Viet Minh fighters were hiding out in the forests along the border.

Ho Chi Minh formed bands of guerrilla fighters to combat the Viet Cong. Guerrilla warfare was effective because of its structure. Guerrilla warfare includes hit-and-run attacks, ambush, raids, and sabotage. Guerrilla fighters, although much smaller in number than professional state military armies, had a number of advantages. They had the ability to be quicker and had better mobility. They had no organized attack. Instead, their attacks were very chaotic, but that did not mean they didn't know what they were doing.

Guerrilla fighters, knowing that they are always greatly outnumbered by the professional state army, conducted attacks on vital areas, such as supply lines, storage areas, and all things that fuel the army. This forces the army to either retreat or slowly die out. This increases chances of victory for the guerrilla fighters and minimizes their own casualties by a large percentage.

This meant that American soldiers were put in harm's way without the ability to wage a fair fight. During Kennedy's presidency, Kennedy did his best to keep the United States out of the war. After his assassination, however, in 1963, and when Vice President Lyndon Baines Johnson became president, he pulled America into war. Before troops were sent to battle the North Vietnamese, severe bombing campaigns were carried out all over North Vietnam. The campaign was called Operation Rolling Thunder.

Before the United States sent troops into Vietnam, the United States Navy was already involved in the fight against communist North Vietnam. Then, on March 8, 1965, 3,500 U.S. marines landed on China Beach. Their purpose was to defend the American air base at Da Nang. They also grouped with 25,000 "advisers," as Kennedy called them, who were already there.

Under communist leader Mao Tse-tung, China supplied the North Vietnamese with weapons and bullets free of charge. Other resources sent from China to the Viet Minh included tanks and munitions. Estimates show that at least five thousand Soviet troops were also supplied to North Vietnam. Those troops shot down USAF aircraft, suggesting an act of war against the United States. The United States did not declare war on the Soviet Union, though, for a number of reasons. They were already deep into the fight with North Vietnam, and the Soviet Union was a country too powerful to engage. It was the surest path into another World War. Trump's response to all this back then: What was it all for? In other words, in the event the United States won, what would it get for all its troubles? He couldn't see a clear answer to that.

When General William C. Westmoreland called for another 200,000 troops to assist him in Vietnam, people were rather upset. Doubts rose and support lessened; in fact, it all but evaporated.

As time passed, reporters witnessed severe atrocities committed by American soldiers against the North Vietnamese. One such incident occurred when a reporter watched as a small boy with a bullet wound in his foot crawled over to a pile of corpses in search of his mother. An American soldier then walked up and fired at him with a machine gun, which sent him flying in the air. The reporter did not notice even a hint of remorse, sadness, or pain. It looked as if the soldiers were enjoying the killing. If not that, then they were indifferent to it.

The war had changed the men who fought in it.

These men who had been someone's father, brother, or son were altered deeply and irreversibly. It was all playing out in front of Trump's eyes, and he did not support any of it.

President Trump has always had a unique sense of loyalty. Just because it does not conform to the sense of most parochial minds or minds that are too caught up with the opposition doesn't mean that he is not the best person to do the job.

You must remember that Donald Trump has been someone who is very straightforward with his intentions. When it came to the war, he felt strongly about it and thought he had better things to do than go and get involved in a war that posed no danger to America. He was not even keen to go to college, as he felt his skills were better utilized by getting to work. But he went to please his father and get the brand of an Ivy League institution alongside his name. What would be the benefit of fighting in a war halfway around the world where there was no threat to America? Nothing. Besides, his deferments were legitimate, and his medical issue was verified and legitimate as well.

Chapter 10 The Relationships

We all have loyalties. Some of us are loyal to our employer, while others are loyal to our parents. Many are loyal to their spouses, but what is loyalty? Why does it color much of our existence? It turns out that all creatures have a certain kind of loyalty. If one observes a colony of ants, a certain kind of loyalty is inherently involved in the structure of that colony.

If you observe a Black Widow spider, there is a strange loyalty that the male engages in after mating. He allows the female to devour him so that his progeny, which she is carrying, has nutrition to carry on the genetic line. That same female spider then allows her young ones to devour her as food.

Nature is full of stories about loyalty in some form or other. Many observers of the Black Widow see it as an act of betrayal to eat the male after copulation, but it is not an act of betrayal by the female but rather the act of loyalty by the male and the adherence to a higher purpose by the female. In the end, the male and the female survive through their offspring.

It's all how one looks at it.

In the same way, different people look at loyalty in different ways. At the level that Trump sees himself, he sees loyalty in a very evolved way. His loyalty concerns such things as life and honor. He applies loyalty to areas that are more critical rather than those that are inconsequential. For instance, it is more important for the greater good for the foot soldier to be loyal to the commander and the king than for the king or the commander to be loyal to the foot soldier.

His first loyalty was to his father. That loyalty was the fruit of great admiration and based on natural forces. Most children are loyal to their parents, and that is part of nature, but in the case of President Trump, his loyalty was a deep bond that was beyond anything that could be described. At the same time, it was not something that could be compared to the way others may define it.

Many imply that loyalty to the country comes first, then loyalty to religion, and then to family, but when the time comes, if they had to choose family over the dictator of a country, it is almost certain that they would choose family first. How is that wrong? It's not. The reason why many scream from the mountaintops that it needs to be a certain way is because they pontificate hypocritically. Trump is straightforward on matters that are this serious.

His loyalty is to his family. The symbol of that loyalty is found in the way he builds the family name. His loyalty to his family name was so pronounced that when his first son was born he was hesitant to name the child after himself.

When his first wife asked why not, he answered that he was concerned that the boy would amount to nothing, and that would tarnish the family name.

His pattern of loyalty can be seen in the life he has led. It can be gleaned from the relationships he has had and his friendships.

Donald Trump started dating early. Even though he was in an all-boys school, he was not one to shy away from girls, and there is nothing wrong with that. He had a healthy adolescent period and found that dating women gave him a sense of balance. There is only one thing that you could say about Trump—"boys will be boys."

Out of the hundred or so people that Trump has dated, it would be exhausting to just list them and look at the kind of woman and manage a sampling of women who have succumbed to his charm.

Some of the more interesting names include Candice Bergen (of *Murphy Brown* fame), who dated Trump when he was about eighteen years old. She was attending the University of Pennsylvania, and Trump was still at NYMA. They dated but couldn't find the spark, and so Trump moved on and so did she. It didn't bother him at all because Trump enjoyed the activity. It wasn't always about the conquest. Many times Trump just wanted to hang out. Whether or not that led to anything was not always the concern. He only experienced magic with a handful of women.

The first ones who really swept him off his feet were his first wife and true love at the time. She eventually became the mother of three of his children, and they had a long and happy marriage. People change, however, and when they do, they do not always change along the same trajectory as their partner.

There is nothing wrong with moving in different directions. It is not easy to stay married when the arcs of growth no longer converge. For a man who is singularly focused on building the family name and altering the face of the business world, hanging around when the other person has gone a different way is not entirely logical or reasonable.

To most people, that is never the issue. They don't see it that way and would not understand, but neither strategy is wrong. Whether someone stays in a marriage after the flame has ended or moves on is neither wrong nor cruel. It is what it is. Judging Trump for having an affair during a marriage is disingenuous. One never can tell what the reasons are for the flame to die down.

This is an element of his honesty—he is not the kind of person who is unclear about the real state of things. The moment the flame is gone, he moves on. When he and his first wife grew apart, he started dating others, but he never neglected his responsibilities. He continued to support her and the children. He was always there for his children.

He dated his second wife soon after the relationship was not as close as it was when they were first married. Ivana, who was a successful businesswoman and a model in her own right, had worked closely with Donald on projects he was working on, and it is not hard to see how that could make things fall apart. The two of them had three children together—Donald Jr., Ivanka, and Eric.

When Ivana and Donald moved apart, he started dating Marla Maples. She was also a model and brilliant in her career. The two married and had a child soon after. In this second marriage, he has one daughter, Tiffany. That marriage was happy for less than a decade, and then the flame died out, and Marla saw something better in Donald's bodyguard. Whether it was something serious or just a fling, we will not know, but that ended the marriage, and Marla and Tiffany moved to California. When they left each other, it was an amicable settlement, and not one of his ex-wives or girlfriends for that matter ever speaks ill of him. That alone says something.

Once that marriage was over Trump, soon dated Kara Young, an accomplished model. It never mattered what race a person was, but it is important to note that Kara is biracial. It is important to mention that because there have been so many accusations that Trump is a racist and a bigot. Dating someone who is half black is the opposite of being a bigot or being racist. It just can't fall into that definition. If people thought about it, they would see that Trump is not a racist, and if he feels that he can't condemn any set group of people that is because he has been a person who tries to bring people together and allow everyone to have their say. That is the meaning of a democracy.

Two of Trump's ex-wives were foreigners when he married them. The only characteristic that seems to be a prerequisite for Donald is that the women he dates are industrious and talented. He also enjoys attractive women. He keeps himself groomed, and he likes his ladies to be well-groomed as well, which is probably why his ex-girlfriends include a number of models.

Some of the other women he dated before finally meeting, dating, and marrying his present wife, Melania Knauss, were Kylie Baxx, a New Zealand model, and Allison Gianni, a popular actress in the '90s. He also dated Rowanne Brewer Lane; Gabriel Sabatinia, a top tennis star from the '90s; and Carla Bruni, who eventually went on to marry ex-French President Nikolas Sarkozy.

There are many more, but the point to take from this without having to go through every one of them is that they all had a good time with him, and they all attest that he behaved like a perfect gentleman.

There is another facet to loyalty that most people do not fully appreciate. They see Donald Trump as someone who will drop you when you no longer serve his purpose. That is not necessarily true. It may seem that way, but that doesn't always happen.

Take, for instance, his loyalty to General Mike Flynn, his first National Security Advisor. Flynn may have had his own agenda in forming national policy, but Trump's entire laundry list of troubles started with the unwillingness that he showed in getting rid of him after Acting Attorney General Sally Yates approached the White House Counsel and warned them about Flynn. The whole problem with the Special Counsel started when he asked the Director of the FBI to lay off the investigation of Flynn. Would a person who is not loyal to his supporters and advisors stick his neck out for them? Not really.

Trump is a straight shooter and always looking for people who are competent and can shoot straight as well, which is one of the reasons why he liked Steve Bannon the first time they met and eventually asked Bannon to take over as the de facto campaign chairman.

He had no loyalty to Manafort because he always thought Manafort was a loser and had no clue as to what he was doing. Trump long suspected that Manafort was in it for himself.

Trump noticed early on that Manafort was not doing what he thought he could. Trump had seen him on TV and realized he was incompetent. He had no personality and no charisma. As time passed, more and more of Trump's patience with his campaign chair evaporated until there was almost none left.

At a gathering at one of Trump's golf properties in New Jersey, the group, including Bannon, Roger Aisles, and Manafort, met to discuss recent coverage they were getting in the *New*

York Times. There was a leak in the Manafort team, and Trump decided that was enough. Everyone, from Rebekah Mercer to Bannon, including Trump, thought Manafort had done a poor job of running the campaign. Little did they know that his primary goal was to send information back to his Russian partner. Whatever they were planning, Manafort had not told Trump about it. That's the reason Manafort managed to get a job with the campaign. He promised to work for free.

When the time came, Trump had no inclination to show loyalty to Manafort the way he had put himself on the line for General Flynn. The defining moment concerning Flynn and Manafort was the degree to which each supported Trump wholeheartedly and with a resounding voice. If you recall the campaign, Flynn was the man who led the crowd in the "Lock her up" chant. That bought him a lot of loyalty with Trump. Compared to that, Manafort didn't do anything that came close.

Chapter 11 The Road Less Traveled

Not many people decide to run for the highest office in the land. Even fewer succeed. It is an exclusive club that consists of forty-four white men and one of mixed heritage. Trump does not have a racist bone in his body. He can be whoever he needs to be to win the moment. In this case, he needed to be the man that despised President Obama. That was what the base needed to see, and that is what he had to do to get the job. He was interviewing for the highest job in the land.

Trump knew more than anyone else that for as much as President Obama was popular, there was a groundswell of other people, the people Kellyanne Conway called "the hidden Trump voter." These were the people no pollster would ever pick up because they were on the fringe—the periphery of the political landscape. That periphery is a metaphor for both their politics and their demographics.

Trump already knew this instinctively, however, long before the likes of Bannon, Conway, and Priebus ever decided they would be there to propel the campaign forward.

Trump always knew that he wanted to be president. It dates back to around the time he attended the New York Military Academy. Trump saw himself as the perfect candidate to be a president that altered the course of history, the kind of man that would one day be on something as grand as Mount Rushmore. Not only did he believe that he could be president, but he also believed strongly and deep down in the soul of his being that he could be one of the greatest presidents the country has ever seen.

In fact, if there is anyone who can do it, or be it, he's the one. He has all the traits of a statesman, but the narrative has taken a turn for the worse. The irony has been that the man who is an expert at branding could not foresee that his entry into the race would come with a branding exercise that altered his name adversely.

His uncommon way of handling this has been sorely misunderstood and frankly become a distraction to everyone. It has become a distraction to him, his staff, and the rest of the country. The truth, however, is that his road to the White House began when he was a teenager. But once again, he had something to do, and so he put off politics. He was not interested in putting aside the work he had to do to improve his father's business.

The notion resurfaced numerous times over the years. He had considered running as a Democrat, an independent, and he had even tried to run as a Republican at one point. He even thought of mounting a third-party bid. The idea that the 2016 election was the only time that candidate Trump had ever made a run for the office is false. To his credit, he had done exceptionally well each time he tried, but at some point in the process he backed off after he decided he wouldn't get the full traction he needed.

The first time it was suggested that Trump run for president was back in 1987. The presidential election in 1988 saw George H.W. Bush run against Michael Dukakis and win. In 1987, rumors started to bubble to the surface that Donald Trump was interested in the position. They were wrong. He had been interested for some time. It was just the first opportunity for him to throw his hat into the ring. He had come out and publicly declared that he had no intention of running, but upon being approached with the idea, he had gone ahead and changed his party affiliation. He resigned from the Democratic party and registered as a Republican.

Trump's political ideologies have always been fungible. He could represent the most liberal of the spectrum one day and the absolute evangelical conservative the next. He could be whoever you wanted him to be as long as there is something in it for him. In most cases, that is the best kind of politician to have. Ideologues are not the best people to do the job.

Politicians who are ideological in nature can

never really understand what the other side is talking about and can never really represent the greatest number of people possible. A person who is fungible, however, can find the greatest number of people who have a common cause and jump on that effectively. Holding political office should be a professional position where you are there to represent the will of the people, not your own will.

When he was considering a run in 1987, he was approached by Mike Dunbar, a political activist. Dunbar had scoured the field of Republicans and was not able to find a suitable candidate to step in following Ronald Reagan's second term.

The only person in Dunbar's sights happened to be a young, successful star by the name of Donald Trump. When Dunbar came knocking, Trump had just turned forty-one and was at the top of his game. He knew how to make an entrance, and he knew how to prop himself up in the public eye. He was as charming as a young Rockefeller but with an older Rockefeller's experience. He knew the value of publicity. At Dunbar's invitation, he arrived in New Hampshire in his large imported helicopter. The arrival was well choreographed. Today, arriving by private jet or private helicopter is not particularly noteworthy, but back then it was something else.

Dunbar was an experienced political operative. He had been the chairman of three successful campaigns in the past, and his keen eye told him that this 41-year-old was a good bet for the office.

Trump was in New Hampshire that day to meet a group of Rotarians who had gathered at a local diner to hear him speak. It was organized by Dunbar and meant to see the response he would get from an early primary state. The response was good. He entertained the thought but backed off as soon as he realized that it was not a winner.

Donald Trump is the kind of man who doesn't take up losing propositions. If he thinks something will not win the day, he will back off. In 1987, he weighed his options and didn't see a clear path forward, so he stepped away from the run.

What was clear, though, even back then was the rhetoric that Trump still echoes today, and more so during his campaign, that Washington and those in it didn't know what they were doing. Trump had been watching politicians for some time. He is very adamant about the way the country is being run and that America has given up its position of strength and leadership.

Weakness is something that Trump never appreciates and never can stomach. When he sees the country capitulate to other foreign powers and do it for no apparent benefit, it bothers him. That holds true today, as it did thirty years ago.

By the time 1988 rolled around, Trump had decided that it wasn't the right time for him to run, and he backed off. He also mentioned that he didn't like the temperament of politics. In the name of checks and balances, opposing forces had made the cauldron of representative government a toxic environment, and he didn't want any part of that. Yet, he took the opportunity to take out an advertisement in three of the East Coast's major publications. He wrote an open letter to the people of the United States titled, "There is nothing wrong with American defense policy that a little backbone can't cure." This was more than thirty years ago, and it clearly articulates Trump's view of the world and of America and its place in the world even today. He has been a true patriot, and he has some ideas about how to do what needs to be accomplished.

Human beings tend to balance and weigh things before making decisions. The decision to move forward on anything is a function of the difference in the opposing forces.

In Trump's case, the force that compelled him to run was not overpowering his hesitancy to run at that point in time. He was riding high in the world. He was doing well, and it would be counterproductive not to make the most of where he was right at that moment. It was around the time that he had just been on the cover of *GQ* magazine. It was also around the time that his casinos were doing well. He had broken the Trump stereotype of being just a property man and had moved into an area that elevated his standing in the eyes of the general public.

The casino business was doing really well at that time, and Trump had just realized that he was not limited to just building properties. He could be a conglomerate within himself. He could spread his prowess as a businessman in areas that were beyond just buildings. That was an idea he liked because it made him look like he was the king of all trades. That impression of being the king of all trades was something that Donald Trump covets. It is in his nature. The key to understanding Trump is within this characteristic.

After the 1988 election when Bush Sr. finally won, Trump kept his intentions on a low key, but he waded into the national debate from time to time. His views of the national state of affairs were unique and not in the mainstream. If he stuck to just strictly his views, then there would be no commonality with any side, and he would be unable to rouse a majority to get elected.

This is not the first time that he sided with the politics of the conservative side of the spectrum. As mentioned above, 1987 was the first time. Yet, he maintained his connections to the Democratic platform, and he donated more money to them than he did to the Republican party.

He tried again in 2000. That cycle saw Al Gore

run against George W. Bush. That was the year when the Supreme Court had to weigh in on the Florida recount. In 2000, he realized that the field that was open to him was one where he could emulate the path of Ross Perot, another billionaire who had tried and failed but made headway for others to follow.

This presented a real opportunity for Trump. The road that Perot had paved during his bid for the White House, which had undoubtedly split the conservative vote, had now laid the platform for another third-party candidate's run.

It worked out that the party did make advances even though Perot failed because soon after that legendary wrestler Jesse Ventura became governor in Minnesota under the Reform Party ticket. This was the highest office that was garnered by the Reform Party. When Perot had stood for election in 1992 against Republican George H.W. Bush and Democrat Bill Clinton, he had managed to get almost 20 percent of the popular vote. Considering that the United States has been primarily a two-party democracy since independence, that split in the vote was a pretty jarring exclamation that affected Republicans and Democrats.

Inspired by his headway, Perot wanted to double his efforts for the upcoming election in 1996. He went on to register with the Reform Party with that purpose in mind. When he ran in 1996 under the Reform Party banner, he only managed to get about 9 percent of the popular vote.

The party was doing well until different factions started to devour it from within. Each faction was trying to build the party in their own image, and that fractured the new party.

When Trump was thinking about a run in 2000, it had been at the prompting of Jesse Ventura. Trump explored the possibilities and registered as a member in 1999. He then went ahead and registered in the party's primaries and won in California before he withdrew his name and quit the party. He explained that the party was in a mess. From the outside, it had seemed that all was well, but once he got in and looked around he had found chaos and knew the party wouldn't add up to much. By this time, Jesse Ventura had also decided to call it quits from the party and converted the Minnesota branch of the Reform Party into the Independence Party. He had made the decision and conferred with Trump who prompted him to leave as well. Not long afterward, Trump also left.

This was another example of his character in not wanting to be associated with anything that would drag him down. If the Reform Party had been better organized and the various factions had kept their battles under control, there would have been a real possibility that they could have made a difference in the way Abraham Lincoln had with the Republican Party.

He then pulled back from seeking any party's

nomination until after President Obama was in office and saw the opportunity Mr. Obama's presidency had created. One segment of society absolutely loved him, and another had nothing but negative feelings about him. In part, that was because of all the hateful talking points that had been spread. Remember that lady in Minnesota who rose and praised Senator McCain and then said she wasn't going to vote for that "Arab" Obama? She had a totally skewed view of who then Senator Obama was. The late Senator McCain had to gently tell her that Obama was "a decent, family man" and that he was not an Arab. Senator McCain only managed to tell that to one woman, but there were millions more like her who didn't get to see that incident and didn't get to hear what Obama was or what he was doing.

The hatred was instinctual.

There was already a groundswell in the conservative community of misinformation about President Obama. The moment Trump saw this was the case, he decided that 2012 would be a good time for him to enter the race. His original platform of giving the country a little backbone was meant to rouse the people who would support such a measure, and it nicely covered all the Republican talking points. But there was one more aspect. The more he kept taunting the current president with the issue of the birth certificate, the more the fringe, who had the same erroneous belief that President Obama was an "Arab," would respond to him.

This was also around the same time that he had called for the meeting with Bossie and Bannon in Trump Tower. He instinctively felt that the time was right again to ride the wave of discontent into the White House. He knew it was the right strategy, and it was a brilliant stroke as well. The more he kept insisting that Obama produce his long form birth certificate, the more he began to resonate with the base that the polls were not picking up. By pressing the issue, he showed that he was a man with their interest at heart. That strategy would only work if President Obama didn't produce the document but kept ignoring the request. The more he did this, the more the fringe base felt that Trump was on the right track.

If President Obama had produced it right away and then produced his transcripts, it would have diffused the whole matter right away, and there would have been no fodder for the fire.

Conclusion

When someone who is an agent of change and destined to shatter the status quo comes along, proponents of the way things are will put up a fight. That fight is not going to be between the ideologues on the Left or Right but rather between those who champion the status quo and those who are forcing change.

The attacks that President Trump is facing and the constant barrage of "presidential harassment" that he endures is not because he is an ineffective leader. Rather, it is because he is someone who has rattled the core of the way things have been. For thirty years, citizen Trump has had a very specific solution for America's problems. You can see it in action today as he brings to life all the ideologies that fuel his foreign policy initiatives.

In that open letter of September 1, 1987, he suggested that the "swamp"—to use his 2016 nomenclature, referring to the elites of Washington, D.C.,—had no spine in the way they dealt with other countries that were taking advantage of America and diminishing our interests.

He wrote, "There is nothing wrong with

American foreign policy that a little backbone can't fix." That was a shot across the bow for the elites who had taken America into countless wars with no clear benefit in sight. When there was a benefit that they could take, we didn't take it and left it for some nebulous and ephemeral gain to be cashed in sometime in the future—a future that never came.

He went on to insinuate a zero-sum world where we are worse off when they are better off. In some ways, that is right, especially when we have policies that allow them to do better at our expense. He said, "For decades, Japan and other nations have been taking advantage of the United States."

He was referring specifically to the war that was taking place in the the Middle East. "The saga continues unabated as we defend the Persian Gulf, an area of only marginal significance to the United States for its oil supplies, but one upon which Japan and others are almost totally dependent. Why are these nations not paying the United States for the human lives and billions of dollars we are losing to protect their interests?" If you listen closely, metaphorically speaking, you will see that Trump has similar thinking today, and it happens to resonate advantageously with his base.

He is of the frame of mind that weaker countries and less-developed countries were not acquiescing to the United States even after taking our assistance when he said, "Saudi

Arabia, a country whose very existence is in the hands of the United States, last week refused to allow us to use their mine sweepers (which are, sadly, far more advanced than ours) to police the Gulf. The world is laughing at America's politicians as we protect ships we don't own, carrying oil we don't need, destined for allies who won't help.

Over the years, the Japanese, unimpeded by the huge costs of defending themselves (as long as the United States will do it for free), have built a strong and vibrant economy with unprecedented surpluses. They have brilliantly managed to maintain a weak yen against a strong dollar. This, coupled with our monumental spending for their, and others, defense, has moved Japan to the forefront of world economies.

Now that the tides are turning and the yen is becoming strong against the dollar, the Japanese are openly complaining, and, in typical fashion, our politicians are reacting to these unjustified complaints. It's time for us to end our vast deficits by making Japan, and others who can afford it, pay. Our world protection is worth hundreds of billions of dollars to these countries, and their stake in their protection is far greater than ours. Make Japan, Saudi Arabia, and others pay for the protection we extend as allies.

Let's help our farmers, our sick, our homeless by taking from some of the greatest profit machines ever created—machines created and nurtured by us. Tax these wealthy nations, not America. End our huge deficits, reduce our taxes, and let America's economy grow unencumbered by the cost of defending those who can easily afford to pay us for the defense of their freedom. Let's not let our great country be laughed at anymore."

With that full page ad that he took out in the major newspapers, spending close to $100,000 on it, he laid open his heart and policy priorities. One just has to replace the names of countries with whoever is taking advantage of us now in his mind.

Donald Trump takes his job seriously. That much is clear but sorely misunderstood. He is unconventional in almost every way one can think of, and he doesn't behave or think like any of the politicians who have preceded him or possibly even many of those who will come after him.

If nothing else, remember that President Trump is a disruptive force that changes the status quo—much like the Steve Jobs, Elon Musks, and Vanderbilts of the world. He is a force that has no patience for weakness and pleasantries in the face of more pressing matters. He is a visionary in the midst of complacency and a leader with a keen sense of what we need as a country.

Lightning Source UK Ltd.
Milton Keynes UK
UKHW011205281019

352454UK00002B/857/P

9 781950 010394